Ghost Towns of Arizona

GHOST TOWNS
OF ARIZONA

By

James E. and Barbara H. Sherman

Maps by Don Percious

Norman

University of Oklahoma Press

International Standard Book Number: 0–8061–0842–8 (cloth); 0–8061–0843–6 (paper)

Library of Congress Catalog Card Number: 68–31367

Copyright 1969 by the University of Oklahoma Press, Publishing Division of the University. Manufactured in the U.S.A. First edition, 1969; second printing, 1970; third printing, 1971; fourth printing, 1972.

To Our Parents

Preface

This book is to be read for fun. We have tried to steer clear of technical mining statistics and figures which would only encumber a book of this type. Our objective is to present brief sketches of the towns, their people, and events from their histories, enhanced by many old and present-day photographs, advertisements and artistic maps.

Some towns left long and detailed histories, while others left few or no accounts of their lives. Consequently we were selective. By no means have we attempted to include every ghost town in Arizona, but we have covered the majority.

How historically accurate many of the facts and stories are is anyone's guess. Early histories are often impaired by large gaps in information. Newspapers and business directories issued in any given period may have exaggerated or may have been incomplete, or time may have caused distortions in the memoirs written by old-timers for magazines, manuscripts and articles. We have presented the information as we found it, without elaboration or magnification.

In compiling our material, we visited almost a hundred ghost towns or their sites, collected over fifteen hundred photographs and used the generous facilities of museums and libraries.

We are gratefully indebted to the many who helped to make this book a reality. Our sincere thanks to the Arizona Pioneers' Historical Society, Tucson, and their most competent and efficient librarians, Nova Alderson and Margaret Sparks; to Sharlot Hall Museum, Prescott, and librarians Elva Breckinridge and Dora Heap; to Mohave Pioneers Historical Society, Kingman, and Kermit Edmonds; Historical Museum, Fort Huachuca, and Orville Cochran; Yuma County Historical Society, Yuma, and William Haught of Yuma Territorial Prison

Historical Monument; Arizona Highway Department, and Warren Hill; University of Arizona Special Collections; American Smelting and Refining Company; Arizona Bureau of Mines; U.S. Geological Survey and U.S. Bureau of Mines library facilities, Denver, Colorado; Library of Congress; California State Library; National Archives; and Department of Postal Research.

For contributing information and photographs and for allowing us to rephotograph old pictures, our thanks go to W. C. Babcock, Charles Bronson, Nell Brown, Mrs. Herbert Enderton, James Loghry, Thomas McMichael, Maggie McShan, Mr. & Mrs. Ralph Morrow, Ted Makinson, Donald Quinn, Lillian Sweetland, and Grant Van Tilborg.

Personal thanks to Don Percious, for his excellent maps, Edward F. Ronstadt for his photographic assistance, generous advice, and encouragement; W. A. Mutterer for the darkroom; Jim McBain and Peggy Scholder of Scot Photo for their fine service; Christopher Mathewson whose jeep was indispensable; Professor Sayner for his professional advice and assistance; John Briedis for his traveling companionship; Alvina Rabago, and Richard Macias.

We extend our deepest appreciation to the scores of other individuals throughout Arizona who allowed us to trespass on private property, gave directions, and took of their time to guide us to obscure locations.

Lastly, we thank those authors and publishers whose literary contributions made possible the research for this book.

It is our hope that *Ghost Towns of Arizona* will serve as a valuable guide and provide enjoyable reading to those who are fascinated by Arizona's past.

JAMES E. AND BARBARA H. SHERMAN

Contents

x |

Ghost Towns of Arizona

Introduction

When Arizona's mining, milling and river settlements found their usefulness or reason for existence no longer profitable or purposeful, they slipped into the category of ghost towns. Some of these communities had mushroomed overnight into a hodgepodge of tents and makeshift homes; others had developed over a period of years into tidy, well-planned townsites. Some had served as supply and distributing points; others as shipping centers. Some were the product of mines; others the product of mills. But whatever their design, intent, or purpose, history now relates their stories.

We begin our brief pursuit of the mining and river navigation development with the forty-niners rushing to the California gold fields. In two years an estimated ten thousand gold seekers, unaware of Arizona's abundant mineral wealth, hastily crossed the Colorado River and continued their westward trek.

Not until the Gadsden Purchase was completed in 1853, giving the United States the portion of Arizona south of the Gila River, did this heretofore land of little distinction begin to disclose her mineral resources to the eager fortune seeker.

By 1856, Charles D. Poston had organized the Sonora Exploring and Mining Company and was exploiting the silver mines in the Cerro Colorado district. A little farther southeast the Patagonia Mine had been discovered and by 1860 was being worked by Lieutenant Sylvester Mowry. The Civil War ended the silver mining endeavors in southern Arizona, since removal of the soldiers from Arizona posts left white men exposed to the savagery of hostile Apaches.

Meanwhile, attention shifted to gold. Jacob Snively discovered promising placers along the Gila River in 1858, producing Arizona's first gold rush. Miners swarming the river banks quickly fabricated Gila City, only to have it vanish with the depleted gold. Pauline Weaver, noted pioneer mountain man, triggered a second boom when he and his party found gold near the Colorado River. La Paz, born in 1862, likewise died a victim of poverty.

Gold was not limited to the easily accessible river banks. The A. H. Peeples party, guided by Pauline Weaver, discovered the Rich Hill bonanza in 1862. A year later the courageous Joseph Reddeford Walker and his party discovered placers in the heart of the Bradshaw Mountains on Lynx, Big Bug, Grooms, and Hassayampa creeks, and the intrepid Henry Wickenburg located his famous Vulture lode.

During the post–Civil War years gold fell to third place and silver and copper took the lead. Prospecting for these two metals resulted in the discovery of silver mines in the Bradshaw, Cerbat, and Tombstone areas, plus the Silver King, McCracken, Stonewall Jackson, Tip Top, and other mines.

The decade of the 1890's pushed gold back into prominence. Some of the gold deposits important during this period were the Congress, Octave, Harqua Hala, La Fortuna, and the King of Arizona.

Since wealth lures people and people require certain commodities, camps began to form. Wherever there was a prosperous mine, group of mines, or a convenient river for milling purposes, the formerly wild country became tame with civilization.

As Arizona's interior sprang to life the Colorado River developed as a major supply route for subsequent debarkation to the inland camps. As a result, river ports began to appear as steamboats started navigating the treacherous Colorado. Castle Dome Landing, Norton's Landing, Ehrenberg, Aubrey Landing, Hardyville, and Polhamus Landing—to name a few—served as vital transferral points for freight, ore, and supplies.

By the turn of the century steamboats were outmoded and railroads had become the leading form of transportation. By this time, also, many of the river landings and interior mining camps had already become ghost towns, no longer requiring the once indispensable services of the steamboat.

New developments in mining technology dawned with the twentieth century. The advent of the electrical age and World War I increased our demand for copper and other critical base metals. Copper reigned as king, pushing such towns as Twin Buttes, Silverbell, Johnson, and Jerome into their peak years. The economic depression beginning in 1929 dethroned copper and left another trail of ghost towns.

This brief glance at mining trends and river landings sets the scene for the birth, life, and death of each settlement mentioned in this book. Inevitable by-products of the development of gold, silver, copper, and other mineral deposits existing in Arizona, these towns exemplify man's innate courage, tenacity, and perhaps even foolishness in his unending search for new frontiers of wealth.

To the Reader

The special format of Ghost Towns of Arizona *was designed for convenient reference. The towns appear in alphabetical order, from Alamo Crossing to White Hills, and along with the page number is printed the alphabetical letter of the towns on that page.*

Directly under the name of each town is listed the county in which it is located, the direction and distance in miles from the nearest present-day town, the page number of the map upon which the ghost town is located, and the date when the first post office was established, and when it was discontinued.

Alamo Crossing

COUNTY: *Mohave*

LOCATION: *about 60 mi. northwest of Wicken-*
burg on Bill Williams River

MAP: *page 177*

P.O. est. as Alimo, Nov. 23, 1899; Rescinded
Dec. 15, 1900. Re-est. as Alamo, March 30,
1911; discont. Dec. 31, 1918.

Founded by Tom Rodgers about the turn of the
century, Alamo Crossing served as a small mining
community for transient prospectors. At one time
the settlement contained a store and post office.
Legend has it that an Indian poisoned the storekeeper and robbed the store, and that the postmaster, bored with his job, confiscated Uncle
Sam's money and disappeared.

For many years a five-stamp mill was used for
custom milling at Alamo Crossing, but the mines
in the district gradually exhausted their supply of
ore and activity in the camp discontinued. The
town revived for a short time during the manga-
nese boom in the early 1950's.

Alamo—looking across the ruins of a five-stamp mill and present-day Alamo Crossing on the north bank of the Bill Williams River.

Alamo—interior of a stamp mill where gold and silver ores were crushed by the impact of the falling steel hammers.

Alexandra

COUNTY: *Yavapai*
LOCATION: *10 mi. southwest of Mayer*
MAP: *page 189*
P.O. est. as Alexandra, Aug. 6, 1878; discont. March 25, 1896.

Alexandra owed its existence to the famous Peck Mine. In June of 1875, E. G. Peck, C. C. Bean, William Cole, and T. M. Alexander were prospecting in the Bradshaw Mountains. Stopping to drink from a spring, Peck noticed a peculiar rock. He examined the mineralization, and decided to have the sample assayed. It proved to be rich in silver. The Peck claim was located and work begun.

Soon a townsite was laid out in "Peck Canyon" and named Alexandra in honor of Mrs. T. M. Alexander, the first lady visitor to the mine.

A winding mountain road was built to remote Alexandra. Prescott became the camp's supply depot, mail routes were established, and the townspeople soon constructed between seventy-five and

Aztlan Mill, 1876. Located on Groom Creek, the Aztlan Mill crushed ore from the Peck Mine and others in the vicinity.—*Courtesy Sharlot Hall Museum*

Alexandra, September 3, 1903. Dedication of a new shaft at the Peck Mine. Among the special committee from Prescott are: (1) Congressman Gobel from Kentucky (2) Congressman Jackson from Ohio (3) Governor Myron H. McCord, thirteenth territorial governor of Arizona (4) Congressman Southard from Ohio.—*Courtesy Sharlot Hall Museum*

Bradshaw Basin, 1880. Advertisement for custom milling from *Arizona Miner* newspaper—note that C. C. Bean, one of the discoverers of the Peck Mine was agent for the Bradshaw Basin Mill.—*Courtesy Arizona Pioneers' Historical Society*

a hundred buildings. There were stores, saloons, boarding houses, livery stables, a blacksmith shop, a butcher shop, and a brewery.

At first the ore was transported by pack train over rugged mountain trails and reduced at the Aztlan Mill. This proved to be both tedious and expensive, since the mill was located some thirty-five miles from the Peck Mine. A ten-stamp mill was installed at the mine by December, 1877, but it never did get much use. As a result of litigation problems which began in 1879 and dragged on and on, the mine was closed. People lived on hope for a while, then left.

Nothing remains of the former mining camp. A mile east of the Peck Mine and just below the site of Alexandra the deserted Swastika Mine buildings cling to the mountain slope. These buildings were constructed during the present century and on occasion have been mistaken for Alexandra.

PRECOTT.

BRADSHAW

BASIN MILL!

READY TO HANDLE FREE OR BASE MILLING ORES
from one ton to any quantity.

ORES WILL BE WORKED
....AT....
Reasonable Rates!
dependent somewhat upon quantity; grade, baseness and expense of treatment. The most

COMPETENT SKILL
will be employed and

Satisfaction Guaranteed!!

☞ Ores taken at dump pile, if desired.
☞ Pack Trains supplied.
☞ Sacks Furnished.
☞ Etc., Etc.

Part'es having ores reduced at this mill are invited and expected to be presen to take their own pulp sample.
C. C. BEAN, Agent.
Dec. 23, 1880.

Alexandra, *circa 1880's— Courtesy Sharlot Hall Museum*

Advertisement.—*Courtesy Arizona Pioneers' Historical Society*

Advertisement.—*Courtesy Arizona Pioneers' Historical Society*

Popularly known as "Allen's Side" or "Allen's Camp," the small settlement was officially referred to as Allen or Quijotoa City. The latter name is not to be confused with the four townsites (Logan City, New Virginia, Brooklyn, and Virginia City) forming the community of Quijotoa to the east.

Populated largely by miners, Allen contained half a dozen houses and a few tents. Nothing remains of the camp.

Allen

COUNTY: *Pima*

LOCATION: *50 mi. southeast of Ajo*

MAP: *page 185*

P.O. est. as Allen, July 5, 1882; discont. Jan. 11, 1886.

General John Brackett Allen, a native of Maine, was an Arizona pioneer. His name is mentioned in connection with the business life of Tucson, Tombstone, Bisbee, and Gunsight. In the early 1880's when people were rushing to the site of the Quijotoa gold and silver boom, General Allen was one of the first men on the scene. Looking over the proposed townsites of the Quijotoa mining community on the east side of Ben Nevis Mountain, he decided that the best site for a hotel would be on the west slope. Accordingly, John Allen erected a hotel at his chosen spot, about six miles by wagon road from Quijotoa. His hotel became known for setting one of the finest tables and serving the choicest liquors in the territory.

John Brackett Allen (1818–99), former territorial treasurer of Arizona, resided in Tucson for twenty-two years.—*Courtesy Arizona Pioneers' Historical Society*

American Flag

COUNTY: *Pinal*
LOCATION: *5 mi. southeast of Oracle*
MAP: *page 193*
P.O. est. as American Flag, Dec. 28, 1880; discont. July 16, 1890.

Located in the late 1870's by Isaac Lorraine, the American Flag Mine was the first in the district to be extensively developed. The mine supported a small camp where a post office was established under the name of American Flag. The Richardson Mining Company of New York bought the property in 1881 and employed forty men. By 1884 the population had dwindled to a reported fifteen. Little was heard of the mine or camp after this time. Isaac Lorraine turned his attention to cattle and established the American Flag Ranch.

Advertisement.—*Courtesy Arizona Pioneers' Historical Society*

F. X. Aubrey, Pathfinder

Aubrey Landing

COUNTY: *Mohave*
LOCATION: *2 mi. northeast of Parker Dam*
MAP: *page 177*
P.O. est. as Aubrey, Oct. 2, 1866; discont. Nov. 3, 1886.

François Xavier Aubrey (b. Maskinonge, Canada, 1824; d. Santa Fe, New Mexico, 1854) was a pioneer trapper and hunter. Because of an event in 1850, he received both fame and the nickname "Skimmer of the Plains." On a thousand-dollar wager that he could do it, Aubrey rode horseback from Santa Fe, New Mexico, to Independence, Missouri, in eight days. Spurred on by success, he later repeated this same eight hundred-mile ride in less time. Aubrey's short life was brought to an abrupt end by Major Richard H. Weightman during an argument and stabbing in a Santa Fe saloon.

A river landing founded at the mouth of the Bill Williams River ten years after Aubrey's death was named in his honor. Aubrey Landing became an important distributing point for the southern part of Mohave County, and freight and supplies were landed there for the McCracken and Sandy districts.

Although Aubrey Landing was believed to be ideally located, the town never grew to its anticipated size. The break in the copper market in 1865 left the place almost abandoned; however, enough stragglers remained to warrant a post office the following year. By 1878 the sights of Aubrey Landing were few but varied. In addition to the assorted piles of copper ore and slag left from the smelting furnaces, there was a combination post office, hotel, store, and saloon under one roof, and an old ship's cabin where W. J. Hardy, an agent for Colorado Steam Navigation Company, resided.

Aubrey Landing supported a small number of people for nearly a decade longer. Now nothing is left of the town.

François X. Aubrey (1824–54), from Ralph E. Twitchell, *Leading Facts in New Mexico History*. Cedar Rapids, Iowa, 1912.

Above—Aubrey Landing. Possibly an early photo-
graph of Aubrey Landing looking south toward the
Buckskin Mountains in Yuma County.—*Courtesy
Yuma Territorial Prison Museum*

Left—Advertisement, 1878. Steamers were in operation along the Colorado River between 1851 and 1877.
—*Courtesy Arizona Pioneers' Historical Society*

Bellevue

COUNTY: *Gila*
LOCATION: *5 mi. southwest of Miami*
MAP: *page 191*
P.O. est. as Bellevue, July 30, 1906; discont.
    April 7, 1927.

Foundations of a gravity-fed mill and scattered
wood from collapsed buildings are all that remain
of Bellevue.

Supported by the Gibson Copper Mine, Bellevue came into existence in the early years of this
century. Once the town and neighboring vicinity
reported about three hundred inhabitants. A
boardinghouse, a general store, the Bellevue-
Miami Stage Line, and the post office were some
of the necessary establishments.

Bellevue townsite was located above and west
of the Gibson Mine, affording an impressive view
of the surrounding area.

Bellevue. Present-day ruins of the gravity feed mill
at the Gibson Mine. Copper ore fed into the crush-
ers at the top of the foundations went down the
hill, through various grinding phases to the flotation units below.

Bellevue, *circa* 1912. Gibson Mine and hoist.—*Courtesy University of Arizona, Special Collections*

Big Bug

COUNTY: *Yavapai*
LOCATION: *12 mi. southeast of Prescott*
MAP: *page 189*
P.O. est. as Bigbug, March 31, 1879; changed to Red Rock, Nov. 28, 1879; changed to Big Bug, March 29, 1881; changed to Bigbug, Aug. 22, 1895; discont. March 31, 1910.

Not even a short history of Big Bug would be complete without mentioning Theodore Boggs, a pioneer settler. Boggs came from an interesting background. His father, a former governor of Missouri, had driven the Mormons out of the state in 1846. His mother was a granddaughter of Daniel Boone. When Theodore Boggs was about ten years old, he traveled to California with the ill-fated Donner party. From California he came to Arizona in 1862. After prospecting for a while in what is now Yavapai County, Boggs settled on Big Bug Creek. Here he continued to prospect and mine.

The Big Bug district was still Indian infested in the 1860's, and prospectors had to be constantly on the lookout. During these early years Theodore Boggs and three companions worked on the Big Bug Claim. Since they were spending considerable time at the mine, they dug a shallow opening into the side of the mountain, in which all four could sleep. To afford more shade at the entrance, they constructed a lean-to and covered the top with poles and grass. In order to make his sleeping hours more comfortable, one of the group made himself a crude bedstead, much to the amusement of his hardier friends.

For about a month the four worked at the mine undisturbed by Indians. One morning they were awakened by the alarming bark of their pet dog. When the barks turned to whimpering howls, one of the men jumped up to investigate the source of the disturbance. He saw the dog, with an arrow piercing his side, and several fast-approaching warriors.

The Indians planned to kill the white men by rolling rocks down on top of the dugout, breaking the lean-to. Fortunately for the miners, the bedstead came in handy. While two of the men re-enforced the roof with the bed, the other two began digging portholes on the upward side of the enclosure where many of the braves were standing. As the Indians prepared to close in, the miners finished the portholes and readied their rifles. Not realizing they could be hit from their hillside position, many of the warriors began approaching from behind the dugout. A volley of gunfire followed and two red men fell dead. Taken by surprise, the braves grabbed the bodies of their fallen companions and hastily retreated up the mountain. Here they cremated their dead in sight of the dugout.

Later, when all seemed safe, the four miners emerged from their shelter. They were somewhat shaken by the event, but unharmed.

Theodore Boggs was one of the first settlers along Big Bug Creek, but it was not long before many other people came into the area. Soon the small community of Big Bug was established, and the town was active and lively. About a hundred people lived in and around the vicinity of the camp.

13
B

For a while the post office was at the residence of Theodore Boggs, just a bit east of the town proper. Miss Dawson, the assistant postmistress, distributed the mail on horseback throughout the mining camp and surrounding area.

Big Bug Creek reveals indications of mining activity, but that is all.

Big Bug, *circa* 1890. Hitchcock Boarding House. —*Courtesy Sharlot Hall Museum*

Big Bug, 1895. Big Bug Smelter, where over a million dollars worth of placer gold and silver were smelted during the 1880's and 1890's.—*Courtesy Sharlot Hall Museum*

Big Bug, *circa* 1888. Boggs Mine on Big Bug Creek.—*Courtesy Sharlot Hall Museum*

Bradshaw City

COUNTY: *Yavapai*
LOCATION: *35 mi. south of Prescott*
MAP: *page 189*
P.O. *est. as Bradshaw, July 1, 1874; discont. Dec. 15, 1884.*

When gold was discovered in the Bradshaw Mountains in the early 1860's, many eager prospectors, miners, and other fortune seekers began focusing their attention on the gold and silver wealth of the inner mountain region. To provide for the needs of these people, Bradshaw City was founded on the pine-covered northwest slope of Mount Wasson. At first there was only a cluster of tents, but abundant timber in the district quickly furnished material for more permanent structures. Stores, shops, saloons, restaurants, and eventually two hotels became part of the town. Travelers to Bradshaw City could reach their destination through the courtesy of Simpson, the ore packer who ran a weekly saddle train from Prescott. The distance covered was about thirty miles, and according to Simpson it took two and a half days to reach the mining camp. An alternate route to the town involved arriving at Minnehaha Flat by wagon road from Walnut Grove and then climbing a steep five-mile trail.

By the summer of 1871, speculation ran high in flourishing Bradshaw City. In a year or so, the community anticipated ten to twenty thousand occupants. As is the case with most boom towns, this number was never realized. At one time, there may have been five thousand people.

Nearby Tiger Mine was the mainstay of the town. By the end of 1871 miners were already drifting elsewhere, although work still continued at the Tiger. Sometime during the 1880's Bradshaw City faded into obscurity. Only scars left by the camp can be found today.

Above—Bradshaw City, *circa* 1870. Tiger Mine, one of the earliest in the Bradshaw Mountains. Production during the 1860's and 1870's approximated $50,000 worth of gold and $700,000 worth of silver. —*Courtesy Sharlot Hall Museum*

Bradshaw City, *circa* 1870.— *Courtesy Sharlot Hall Museum*

Bueno

COUNTY: *Yavapai*
LOCATION: *22 mi. south of Prescott on Senator Highway*
MAP: *page 189*
P.O. est. as Bueno, June 27, 1881; discont. June 1, 1893.

Bueno was the mining camp for the Bully Bueno gold ledge. Bob Grooms located the mine on Turkey Creek in the Bradshaw Mountains about 1863 or 1864. Since the ledge was quite extensive and the United States mining laws, at that time, required that a mining location could be only two hundred feet long, several prospectors obligingly took up claims on it. There were sufficient miners, in fact, to form a community large enough to ward off the menacing Indians.

As news of the Bully Bueno spread, the superintendent for the Walnut Grove Gold Mining Company, whose headquarters were in Philadelphia, came to examine the property. Pleased with what he saw, he purchased the mine for the company and erected a twenty-stamp mill. Two men, named Bigoli and Campbell, were left in charge of the property.

Soon afterward, Bigoli and Campbell, while sleeping one night in a log house adjoining the new mill, were awakened by the smell of smoke. Indians had started a fire against the cabin door. Quickly wrenching a shelf from the wall, the two men managed to open the door and push the flaming pile of pine needles and grass away from the building before any damage occurred. After a short time, when the fire had died out and all appeared still, Bigoli decided to sneak out to have a look. Although armed with a shotgun, Bigoli did not get much beyond the cabin. Abruptly he stumbled back, with an arrow quivering in his stomach. Campbell managed to draw out the shaft, but the arrowhead remained lodged deep in the wound. With his companion made as comfortable as possible, Campbell stood guard to watch for more trouble. Two hours later a brave appeared, silently creeping toward the cabin with an armload of dry grass. Campbell shot and killed him.

When dawn disclosed the dead body gone and no Indians in sight, Campbell made a break for Prescott. A party was dispatched to rescue Bigoli, who recovered completely, although the arrowhead never was removed.

The early, dangerous years of the 1860's passed, and by the 1880's Bueno, no longer hampered by the Indians, was an active settlement. Two mills were in operation, gold and silver were shipped, mail arrived semi-weekly, and stages ran between Bueno and Prescott. The population of 250 people supported a general store, meat market, and school, and had in residence a lawyer and a justice of the peace.

No evidence of the camp is visible today.

Bumble Bee

COUNTY: *Yavapai*
LOCATION: *50 mi. north of Phoenix, west of Interstate 17*
MAP: *page 189*
P.O. est. as Bumble Bee, Feb. 3, 1879.

There are various versions of the origin of the name Bumble Bee. About 1860 a small company of cavalry located a temporary post at the present settlement of Bumble Bee. Two possible derivations of the name have been related to this encampment. One story tells that an army scout reported to his superior that Indians were as thick as bumblebees in the area. Another story relates that soldiers mistook the distant noise of an Indian powwow for a swarm of bumblebees. A third version is accredited to a group of early prospectors. While looking for placer gold in the creek bottom they were beset by bumblebees. For whatever reasons, Bumble Bee Creek it was named.

An early stage stop between Prescott and Phoenix was Snyder's Station on Bumble Bee Creek. It was named for W. W. Snyder, a local rancher and horse breeder. When a post office was established there in 1879, the name was officially changed to Bumble Bee.

Although there was gold placer mining in the region, Bumble Bee never boomed as a mining town. Records indicate that it was a small settlement which served as an important stagecoach stop and boasted a general store and a post office.

The buildings of the town were put up for sale in 1949. Today the place is privately owned. Antiques and a group of buildings characteristic of a western frontier town have been constructed as a tourist attraction.

Bumble Bee. Present-day attraction is a frontier street scene display.

Calabasas

COUNTY: *Santa Cruz*

LOCATION: *8 mi. north of Nogales*

MAP: *page 195*

P.O. est. as Calabazas, Oct. 8, 1866; discont. Aug. 31, 1868. Re-est. April 26, 1880; changed to Calabasas, Dec. 19, 1882; discont. Aug. 15, 1913.

The early history of Calabasas reaches far back into Arizona's past. Long before Calabasas became a railroad promoters' boom town, the site had served as a Papago Indian village, a Spanish settlement, a Mexican garrison, a U.S. military base, a mining camp, and a farming community. In the early 1880's, with the westward expansion and the extension of railroads, Colonel C. P. Sykes, owner of the Calabasas Land Grant, saw an opportunity to promote Calabasas as the future gateway into Mexico.

After the Southern Pacific and Santa Fe Railroads were linked at Deming, New Mexico, Santa Fe's plan was to continue their route through Arizona to the Mexican seaport of Guaymas, Sonora. Work on the Mexican end started at Benson, Arizona. Tracks were laid south to Fairbank, then west to the Santa Cruz, and finally south into Sonora, Mexico. The Deming section was still unconstructed, but certainty that it would be built prompted anticipation of the railroad's becoming a transcontinental thoroughfare. Realizing that a settlement undoubtedly would spring up near the border, Colonel Sykes jumped into the act by encouraging Santa Fe promoters to consider the advantages of Calabasas as Arizona's future port of entry into Mexico. Although at that time Calabasas did not amount to much more than a combination country store and post office, a two-story brick building occupied by a saloon, and the United States Custom House, the place appeared to be an ideal location for a new town.

The future city was surveyed, mapped, and extensively but falsely advertised both east and west as a glamorous metropolis on the banks of the Santa Cruz. As the railroad people and other settlers began surging into Calabasas, the old townsite changed its appearance. Many tent saloons sprang up. Three enterprising Chinamen, Cum Sing, Hi Sing and Lo Sing, erected the Palace Hotel, a large tent floored with pine boards and divided by a canvas partition into two rooms, a dining room and a kitchen. The biggest boast and pride of Calabasas was the commodious and modern Santa Rita Hotel, erected at great personal expense by Colonel Sykes. It was supplied with every available comfort. Excellent furniture and carefully selected pictures adorned every room. In October of 1882, the Santa Rita officially opened with pomp and ceremony, and was reported to be the finest hotel between San Francisco and Denver.

Calabasas was the scene of many acts of violence. One of the milder scrapes occurred on a Sunday afternoon in May, 1882. A saloonkeeper from near the Mexican border came to Calabasas and proceeded to indulge in a demonstrative argument with a stranger in front of Smith & Bain's Saloon. A curious crowd gathered to witness the melee, which ended when the saloonkeeper drew his revolver and fired. The bullet penetrated the stranger's arm and then hit a bystander in the ankle. Wasting no time, the saloonkeeper swung onto his horse and left town, with Deputy Sheriff Vosburgh in hot pursuit. After an exciting four-mile chase, the deputy covered the offender and made him give up his side arms and surrender. The captured saloonkeeper was brought back into town and heavily fined for his misdemeanor.

Calabasas' hopes of becoming the gateway city to Mexico were shattered with the establishment of a new border town, Nogales. After enduring a feeble existence into the present century, Calabasas succumbed and vanished.

Calabasas, *circa* 1880. Plans for the Hotel Santa Rita and Plaza at Calabasas. The hotel, built by Mr. Joseph E. Wise in 1882, was destroyed by fire in 1927 or 1928.—*Courtesy Arizona Pioneers' Historical Society*

PLAN OF THE HOTEL AND PLAZA AT CALABASAS AS IT WILL APPEAR WHEN COMPLETED.

Calabasas, 1934. Today nothing is left of these ruins. — *Courtesy Arizona Pioneers' Historical Society*

Castle Dome Landing

COUNTY: *Yuma*

LOCATION: *on the Colorado River about 30 mi. north of Yuma*

MAP: *page 179*

P.O. est. as Castle Dome, Dec. 17, 1875; discont. Dec. 4, 1876. Re-est. as Castle Dome Landing, Aug. 6, 1878; discont. June 16, 1884.

There were indications that ore veins in the Castle Dome Mountains had been worked prior to their discovery by prospectors in 1863. Palo verde and ironwood trees growing in the weathered excavations and on the dumps evinced the antiquity of previous mining activity. Worn paths were found leading south from the workings for some eighteen miles to the Gila River, where there were ruins of adobe furnaces. It was generally believed that Indians had back packed the ore along these trails during the time of the early Spanish explorers.

There was much excitement at first. Many prospectors finding shiny galena thought the veins to be pure silver. Since most of the metallic mineralization proved to be lead ore, the silver fortune seekers became disappointed and left.

In 1864 Castle Dome Landing was founded on the Colorado River. It served as a supply and shipping point for the mines fifteen miles east in the Castle Dome Mountains. The town was the first stop for steamboats traveling up the Colorado River from Yuma. Castle Dome Landing was small, but it was active. During the next two decades the community acquired fifty reported residents, a post office, general store, hotel, saloon, stage agency, smelting furnace, and a justice of the peace.

Work continued sporadically at the mines for many years after the river landing of Castle Dome ceased to exist. Today, the landing site is covered by water impounded by the Imperial Dam.

Castle Dome Landing, 1877. *Courtesy Sharlot Hall Museum*

Catoctin

COUNTY: *Yavapai*
LOCATION: *16 mi. southeast of Prescott*
MAP: *page 189*
P.O. est. as Catoctin, Dec. 29, 1902; discont. July 15, 1920.

Catoctin, a small gold mining camp on upper Hassayampa Creek, never amounted to much. A population of twenty was reported in 1914. Apparently enough miners made a living here to warrant a post office for eighteen years. Two of the mines in the area were the Catoctin and Climax gold mines.

Catoctin, *circa* 1910, Catoctin Mine and camp.
—*Courtesy Sharlot Hall Museum*

Cedar

COUNTY: *Mohave*
LOCATION: *about 60 mi. southeast of Kingman in the Hualapai Mountains*
MAP: *page 177*
P.O. est. as Cedar, Sept. 24, 1895; discont. July 31, 1911.

Located on the east slope of the Hualapai Mountains, Cedar was the mining community for gold, silver, and copper mines in the district. Mines were being worked in the area some twenty years prior to the establishment of the Cedar post office in 1895. In 1907 the Cedar Valley Gold & Silver Company, Yucca Cyanide Mining & Milling Company, and various other mines supported approximately two hundred people. In addition to the post office, there were two saloons and a general merchandise store.

Today, scattered rock ruins, foundations, and indications of mining activity extend along the valley for about half a mile.

Cedar—ruins.

Cerbat

Cerbat, *circa* 1890.—*Courtesy Mohave Pioneers Historical Society*

COUNTY: *Mohave*
LOCATION: *about 10 mi. northwest of King-man east of U.S. 93*
MAP: *page 175*
P.O. est. as Cerbat, Dec. 23, 1872; changed to Campbell, June 25, 1890; changed to Cerbat, Oct. 24, 1902; discont. June 15, 1912.

Mining in the Cerbat range began in the late 1860's. As miners gradually accumulated in the area, Cerbat mining camp began to take shape. Nestled in a remote canyon running west from the mountain range, Cerbat must have seemed isolated in the early days. The town was reached by a three hundred-mile steamboat trip up the Colorado River from Yuma to Hardyville and thence by stage over a wagon road for thirty-eight miles. Nevertheless, the community grew encouragingly enough so that by 1872 there was talk of building a six thousand-dollar road to bring Cerbat occupants closer to Fort Rock, Camp Hualapai, Williamson Valley, Prescott, and civilization.

Cerbat, *circa* 1890. Arrastra used to crush ore—*Courtesy Mohave Pioneers Historical Society*

Cerbat. Between 1871 and 1907 the Golden Gem Mine produced $400,000 worth of gold, silver, lead and zinc. Other important mines that contributed to the support of Cerbat were the Idaho, Flores, Esmeralda, Night Hawk, and Big Bethel.

During the 1870's Cerbat gained high enough status to be made the third seat of Mohave County. Unfortunately, it did not hold this honor for very long; Mineral Park captured the county seat from Cerbat in 1877.

When Cerbat first started developing, the camp was only a few shanties, but it was not long before many buildings were constructed and scores of miners' cabins dotted the surrounding hills. The town boasted the usual merchandise stores, saloons, and shops typical of most mining communities. Other additions were a free school opened for six months of the year and a smelting furnace for gold and silver ore. Two physicians and two lawyers met the personal needs of the hundred or so residents.

Mining prosperity in the Cerbat Mountains kept the town alive into the present century. A few wooden buildings, some rock foundations, assorted rubble, and an obscure cemetery remain today.

Present-day ruins of the Cerbat post office.

Cerro Colorado

COUNTY: *Pima*
LOCATION: *about 55 mi. southwest of Tucson on the Arivaca road*
MAP: *page 195*
P.O. est. as Cerro Colorado, April 17, 1879; discont. April 15, 1911.

By signing the Gadsden Purchase in 1853, the United States acquired the southern portion of Arizona. Two years later the Sonora Exploring and Mining Company was formed. Organized by Charles D. Poston, the company set up headquarters at Tubac and commenced work on the silver mines in the Cerro Colorado district.

The most famous of the mines was the Heintzelman, named for Samuel P. Heintzelman, first president of the Sonora Exploring and Mining Company, who later achieved fame during the Civil War.

Work progressed smoothly at Cerro Colorado until just prior to the outbreak of the Civil War. One day fifteen Mexicans and Indians working deep in the mine became the victims of a mass burial. The mine roof caved in, and there was no way of rescuing any possible survivors. Many of the remaining miners, convinced that the mine was haunted, left Cerro Colorado for their native homeland of Mexico.

The Civil War followed, and military troops were removed from Arizona. The Apaches, believing they had scared away the soldiers in southern Arizona, felt justified in exterminating any remaining white men; consequently, the mining camps were under constant threat of Indian attack. About this time, Charles Poston, required to leave Cerro Colorado on business, left his brother, John, in charge of the mine workings.

Continuous stealing and desertion plagued operations, prompting John Poston to employ extreme measures. After catching his foreman, Juanito, heading south toward Mexico with a load of silver bullion, Poston executed him in the hope that his punishment would serve as an example. Juanito's death only succeeded in further disrupting work at the mine. During the following nights, Mexican miners stole whatever they could, then disappeared to their homes in Sonora. Whether fact or legend, with them went a story about Juanito and how he had buried seventy thousand dollars in stolen silver bullion somewhere near the mine. Mexican outlaws, hearing the tale, immediately headed into Arizona. Reaching Cerro Colorado, they had no difficulty in winning over the remaining Mexican population, after which they brutally murdered John Poston and two German employees. The outlaws then proceeded to tear up the mine workings looking for the buried treasure. They never found it; no one ever has.

In those early days, the village of Cerro Colorado consisted of assorted buildings and storehouses. A walled fortification marked the entrance to the mine, and a tower located in one corner of the town plaza served to protect the workings.

Mining continued intermittently after the Civil War as the hacienda slowly crumbled. During later years other buildings were constructed on the original foundations, but these, too, have deteriorated into ruins.

23
c

Cerro Colorado—only a few crumbled walls remain.

Major General Samuel P. Heintzelman (1805–80). Heintzelman was recommended to West Point by James Buchanan and graduated from the Academy in 1825. In 1850 he established a military post at Fort Yuma and in 1855 he became president of the Sonora Exploration and Mining Co.—*Courtesy Library of Congress*

Cerro Colorado, *circa* 1864, from J. Ross Browne, *A Tour Through Arizona 1864*. New York, Harper & Brothers, 1869.

Cerro Colorado, looking north, as it appears today.

Charles D. Poston (1825–1902) organized the Sonora Exploring and Mining Company in 1855. He was elected from Tucson to the First Territorial Legislature in 1864 and became Speaker of the House.—*Courtesy National Archives*

Cerro Colorado. Grave of John Poston (1830–61), murdered by Mexicans at the Heintzelman Mine.

Chaparral before 1888.
—*Courtesy Sharlot Hall Museum*

Chaparral

COUNTY: *Yavapai*
LOCATION: *4 mi. west of Humboldt*
MAP: *page 189*
P.O. est. as Chaparral, May 24, 1894; discont. Dec. 31, 1917.

Chaparral, a flourishing camp in the 1890's, depended upon the Little Jessie, McCabe, and other gold mines. It was a lively and occasionally a rough town, but it was efficiently kept under control by Deputy Sheriff Mike Enright.

About twenty business concerns supplied the needs of the people. Among these were Louis Beach's Chop and Short Order House, Stillwell and Hobbs Butcher Shop, F. H. Shimer's fruits, tobaccos, and ice cream, Hudgen's Hotel, plus merchandise stores and saloons.

By the turn of the century, Chaparral had been pushed from prominence by the rapidly growing nearby camp of McCabe.

Until the post office was closed in 1917, fifty to seventy-five people composed the camp's population. The town has since disappeared.

Charleston

COUNTY: *Cochise*
LOCATION: *9 mi. southwest of Tombstone*
MAP: *page 195*
P.O. est. as Charleston, April 17, 1879; discont. Oct. 24, 1888.

Hidden among mesquite and cottonwood trees on the west bank of the San Pedro River are the scattered adobe ruins of Charleston. These are becoming fewer and harder to find every year.

Located some nine miles southwest of Tombstone, Charleston served as a milling town for the Tombstone mines. During the 1880's, it was an active and prosperous community containing saloons, hotels, general merchandise stores, restaurants, livery stables, a meat market, hay yard, post office, school, and church, with a blacksmith, physicians, and four hundred other residents.

Once there was an Indian scare when word arrived that Apaches decked in war paint were headed toward Charleston. The townsmen, armed and mounted, rode out to meet the oncoming warriors—but no Apaches appeared.

Some writers describe Charleston as being a wild and wicked place; it may have been. Whether good or bad, the men of Charleston worked hard, and occasionally they had to have their fun—such as the party given by a man named Durkee, who was in charge of freighting ore from Tombstone to Charleston. When Durkee's first year profits exceeded his expectations, he decided to throw a party for the miners. He rented for the occasion a spacious saloon in Charleston, ordered an abundant supply of liquor from the best wines to the cheapest whisky, and hired an orchestra and female entertainers. The party was a noisy, boisterous affair with all inhibitions discarded. The men drank, gambled, laughed, and cussed. Sometime after midnight, a riot broke loose. Tables were overturned, chairs broken, glasses and bottles smashed, and plate glass mirrors shattered. Fortunately, all the men had been searched for guns when they entered the party, so the fighting was confined to the use of fists and brute strength. The next day, Durkee reimbursed the saloonkeeper for the damages and vowed never to throw another party.

Jim Burnett, justice of the peace, was law in Charleston. After Burnett had a disagreement with the Cochise County Board of Supervisors over financial matters, he declared that his court would be run on an independent basis. Burnett would arrest offenders, sentence them on the spot, and pocket all fines. When Jack Swart, a saloonkeeper, killed a man named Chambers, Burnett fined Swart a thousand dollars. He charged a Mexican nine cords of wood for stealing a horse, and then sold the wood to the mill. Cowboy offenders were fined from five to a hundred head of cattle, depending upon the degree of their misdemeanor. Through such transactions as these, Jim Burnett always had enough money.

Occasionally some of the ruffians from Galeyville would come to Charleston to have a good time. One Sunday, such a group arrived in town led by Curley Bill Brocius. After making the rounds of the saloons and getting drunk, they decided to go to the church, where a community service was in progress. As the gunmen filed in, the frightened congregation left their pews and filed out. The minister also tried to make a hasty retreat, but was stopped by a member of the gang who demanded a sermon. The good preacher delivered his sermon and then prayed for their souls, after which the men sang a hymn and one of the outlaws passed a hat among his companions. The collection, given to the preacher, was the largest ever contributed. The next day, Jim Burnett fined Curly Bill twenty dollars for disturbing the peace.

Burnett wound up his career in an abrupt manner. He blasted a dam belonging to William Green, a local rancher. The water swept down the wash and drowned two girls who were fishing in the stream below. One was Green's daughter. Grieved and angered, Green shot and killed Burnett outside the Can Can Restaurant in Tombstone on July 7, 1897.

Flooding of the mines at Tombstone marked the end of Charleston. Work stopped, business establishments closed their doors, the post office discontinued, and people left. By the mid-1890's, the town had been taken over by a Mexican population who set up tents and claimed the deserted buildings.

During World War II, Charleston was used by soldiers at nearby Fort Huachuca as a battleground for war games. These mock fights destroyed much of the remaining town.

Today the only relics of Charleston are disintegrating walls and a neglected cemetery. The cemetery, located about a mile and a half north of Charleston, is difficult to find and little is left of it.

Charleston, 1889.—*Courtesy Arizona Pioneers' Historical Society*

Upper left — Charleston, 1963. Ruins on the west bank of the San Pedro River.—*Courtesy Historical Museum, Fort Huachuca*

Upper right—Judge James Burnett, justice of the peace at Charleston. —*Courtesy Sharlot Hall Museum*

Left—Charleston, 1899—already a ghost town.—*Courtesy Historical Museum, Fort Huachuca*

Lower — Charleston, 1885. *Fly Photograph, Courtesy Arizona Pioneers' Historical Society*

Cherry

COUNTY: *Yavapai*
LOCATION: *31 mi. east of Prescott*
MAP: *page 187*
P.O. est. as Cherry, March 3, 1884; discont. March 15, 1943.

Cherry. Deserted school house.

Now a small, quiet village, Cherry once flourished as an active mining center. Mines in the Cherry Creek district were reported by the late 1870's. In these early years, mule-driven arrastras crushed the rich gold ore. Later, during the peak year of 1907, six mills were in operation. Much of the mining speculation and development during the boom period, however, was the result of promotional campaigns. Over forty mines in the area have had intermittent production.

Cherry and vicinity claimed four hundred inhabitants during its heyday, and customary businesses and professions served the public.

Chilito

COUNTY: *Gila*
LOCATION: *about 8 mi. north of Hayden*
MAP: *page 191*
P.O. est. as Chilito, June 11, 1913; discont. July 15, 1918.

Chilito, *circa* 1947, from George A. Kiersch, *The Geology and Ore Deposits of the Seventy Nine Mine Area, Gila County, Arizona.* (Dissertation, University of Arizona Library, 1947.)

In this vicinity copper ore deposits located about 1880 were eventually sold to the London-Arizona Copper Company. In 1913, as a result of a merger, the name was changed to the London-Arizona Consolidated Copper Company. From that time until 1920 intermittent work on the London-Arizona Mine produced the mining camp of Chilito.

During the early part of 1920, base metal prices soared, encouraging full-scale mining. Chilito appears to have reached a peak at that time, with a population of two hundred. A drop in metal prices at the end of that year brought the period of intense mining operations—and Chilito—to an end.

The buildings and site of Chilito were later used by ranchers.

Christmas. Ruins of the mill where over $9,000,000 worth of copper was concentrated.

Christmas

COUNTY: *Gila*
LOCATION: *9 mi. north of Winkleman*
MAP: *page 191*
P.O. est. as Christmas, June 17, 1905; discont. March 30, 1935.

Two separate copper claims were located in the Dripping Springs Mountains. One location was made by Bill Tweed and Dennis O'Brien in 1878, and another by Dr. James Douglas in 1882. Nothing materialized from these claims, since the land lay within the San Carlos Apache Indian Reservation. Eventually the reservation boundaries were resurveyed. When news about this change reached George Crittenden and N. H. Mellor on Christmas Eve of 1902, they wasted no time, but hurried to the site of the previous discovery. Arriving early Christmas morning, they staked their claims.

The community of Christmas, growing around the mining activities, eventually included a dairy, meat market, barbershop, general merchandise store, Catholic church and school. The town's peak population was probably about a thousand people. During the prosperous years, the little post office was swamped with Christmas cards and letters. Sent under cover from all parts of the United States, these were to be remailed with the Christmas postmark.

The mine was inactive for some years, but reopened for work in 1956. Today Christmas is a combination of the old and the new.

Underground drilling, *circa* 1910. The drill steel is being changed on a compressed air drill. This routine takes place whenever the bit becomes dull or the steel becomes too short.— *Courtesy Arizona Pioneers' Historical Society*

Chrysotile

COUNTY: *Gila*
LOCATION: *37 mi. northeast of Globe, west of U.S. 60*
MAP: *page 191*
P.O. est. as Chrysotile, June 27, 1916; discont. July 15, 1933.

Asbestos mines were located in Ash Creek by the West brothers and Fred Patee in 1913. During the early years of production, burro pack trains were used to carry the asbestos shipments from Ash Creek to the railhead at Globe. In 1916, the property was purchased and further developed by the Johns-Manville Company.

Chrysotile, the type of asbestos mined in Ash Creek, was the name given to the small village which sprang up on the canyon floor. By 1928, the camp consisted of tents and stone houses, a store, blacksmith shop, and power plant. The company employed about 170 men to mine the deposits in the canyon walls.

When Hoover Dam was constructed on the Colorado River in the 1930's, asbestos from these particular mines was used for insulation in the hydroelectric plant.

Some mining continues in Ash Creek Canyon. A few people still live in Chrysotile, but most of the original buildings are gone.

Clarkston

COUNTY: *Pima*
LOCATION: *1 mi. east of Ajo*
MAP: *page 185*
P.O. est. as Rowood, Jan. 21, 1918; changed to Samclark, Feb. 26, 1918 (rescinded). Discont. Nov. 30, 1955.

Sam Clark (born 1871: died 1933) founded the town of Clarkston (Clarkstown) in opposition to Ajo, the New Cornelia Copper camp. The townsite was laid out on a group of mining claims about a mile east of Ajo. By 1916, Clarkston had become the more popular of the two communities with an estimated population of fifteen hundred. There were more than sixty business establishments, including a bank, motion-picture theater, billiard and pool hall, two shower-bath houses, two soft drink stands, the newspaper, *Copper News*, and a milk depot, hardware store, furniture store, and music shop. Sam Clark owned Clarkston and rented lots. Prices ranged up to twenty dollars, depending on whether the property was used for business or living purposes.

The biggest problem was a water shortage, since the New Cornelia Copper Company refused to sell any water to Clarkston's residents. Until a supply was obtained by deepening a shaft, water had to be hauled from elsewhere. Even in the community's peak years, vendors sold drinking water because of the highly mineralized taste of the town's own supply.

In 1918, a post office was established at Clarkston under the name Rowood. The popularity of President Woodrow Wilson had prompted the residents to request either the name Wilson or Woodrow for their new post office. When both names were rejected by the Post Office Department, the people settled for the name Rowood.

Most of Clarkston was destroyed by fire in 1931. The Rowood post office moved to nearby Gibson and continued service for many years.

Clarkston—only a few concrete foundations and ruins mark the site.

Clarkston in 1916, looking east down main street. The large false front building on the right was Levy's Merchandise. In this store, Levy kept a large safe, which robbers forced him to open in or about 1930. The robbers were caught in White's Rooming House, one of Clarkston's first buildings.—*Courtesy University of Arizona, Special Collections*

Sam and Angeline Clark, 1916, in front of their home in Clarkston.—*Courtesy University of Arizona, Special Collections*

Main Street of Clarkston, 1917.—*Courtesy University of Arizona, Special Collections*

Cleator

COUNTY: *Yavapai*
LOCATION: *60 mi. north of Phoenix, west of Interstate 17*
MAP: *page 189*
P.O. est. as Turkey, March 21, 1903; changed to Cleator, May 1, 1925; discont. July 15, 1954.

Cleator used to be called Turkey or Turkey Creek Station; James P. Cleator changed the name. During the early years of this century, Turkey was surrounded by prosperous mines. As the need for better transportation arose, a branch line of the Prescott and Eastern Railroad was constructed between Mayer and Crown King. A year later James P. Cleator arrived at Turkey Creek Station.

James Cleator was born in Ramsey on the Isle of Man in 1870. At thirteen he became a sailor on a fishing vessel and for the next few years sailed extensively. Arriving in America in 1890, Cleator ended his sailing career and turned his attention to mining. He moved around the mines in northern California and British Columbia, eventually making his way to Arizona and to the town that would later bear his name.

L. P. Nellis, postmaster, notary public, and operator of a general store in Turkey Creek Station, owned most of the town in 1905. He and Cleator became good friends and later branched out as partners in cattle ranching. Cleator soon traded his interest in the ranch to Nellis for the town.

James Cleator ran a post office and general store for many years, as the community continued to serve such mines as the DeSoto, Silver Pheasant, and Swastika.

By 1933, the railroad was abandoned, since much of the mining activity had ceased. Cleator was fast becoming a ghost town.

James Cleator, who was getting on in years, put the town up for sale in 1949. At that time there were about twenty houses, a grocery store, service station, saloon, schoolhouse, and sixty residents.

Crown King road, *circa* 1904. Railroad construction between Cleator and Crown King.— *Courtesy Sharlot Hall Museum*

Present-day Cleator, located on the east side of the Bradshaw Mountains.

Clip

COUNTY: *Yuma*
LOCATION: *40 mi. north of Yuma*
MAP: *page 179*
P.O. est. as Clip, Feb. 6, 1884; discont. Oct. 13, 1888.

In the early 1880's, the Silver Clip claim was located. A ten-stamp mill to work the ore was erected on the Colorado River about eight miles northwest of the mine. By 1882, the mill had started production. The community of Clip, including a lively population of about two hundred people, a post office, and a general merchandise store, grew up around the milling complex.

The Silver Clip Mine was operated by men named Hubbard and Bowers until April, 1887. For a while the mill ran on mine tailings, but gradually the work stopped. The population drained from Clip, the post office closed, and the town ceased to exist.

Cochran

COUNTY: *Pinal*
LOCATION: *about 15 mi. east of Florence*
MAP: *page 191*
P.O. est. as Cochran, Jan. 3, 1905; discont. Jan. 15, 1915.

Not only was Cochran a mining camp, but it also served as a station on the Santa Fe, Prescott and Phoenix Railroad. Mines in the area were worked by Copper Butte and Silver Belle mining companies. Inhabitants of the vicinity numbered about a hundred with Cochran supporting a post office, general merchandise store, boardinghouse, and other establishments. John S. Cochran was its first postmaster, hence, the town's name.

Columbia

COUNTY: *Yavapai*
LOCATION: *25 mi. west of Wickenburg*
MAP: *page 189*
P.O. est. as Columbia, Sept. 25, 1894; discont. July 31, 1915.

Situated on Humbug Creek, Columbia, a mining camp of about a hundred people, listed among its establishments and professions a post office, general store, meat market, blacksmith, shoemaker, carpenter, and justice of the peace. Two of the major mining companies were the Acquisition and Tip Top Heath.

Congress

COUNTY: *Yavapai*
LOCATION: *19 mi. north of Wickenburg*
MAP: *page 183*
P.O. *est. as Congress, Jan. 19, 1889; discont. Aug. 31, 1938.*

One of Arizona's most celebrated gold mines, the Congress, was located by Dennis May on March 25, 1884, and three years later bought and developed by Diamond Joe Reynolds, an eastern financier. Reynolds died in 1891 and the mine remained inactive until 1894, when it was purchased by E. B. Gage, Frank Murphy, and N. K. and Wallace Fairbank. As the mine proved profitable, the mining camp of Congress grew and flourished.

Congress had two distinct sections or towns; "Mill Town" and "Lower Town." "Mill Town" contained the mill, hospital, company offices, bunkhouses and homes of the employers and employees. "Lower Town," straggling along the canyon, contained the business establishments and other homes. There were saloons, boardinghouses, both Chinese and Mexican restaurants, meat markets, general merchandise stores, a dry goods store, Catholic and Presbyterian churches, a three-teacher adobe school building, and even a tennis court. Congress also boasted of its telegraph and telephone connections with the outside world and its own electric light plant.

The major drawback at Congress was the scarcity of water. All water for the camp was obtained from a small spigot in front of the company's store in "Mill Town." Each family had a fifty-gallon whisky barrel which could be rolled up the hill to the faucet, filled with water, then allowed to roll down the hill by its own weight. At least twice the lack of water proved disastrous to the "Lower Town." Early on an April morning in 1898, a fire broke out and destroyed nearly all business buildings. Again, in November of 1900, a fire which started in a rooming house behind the Red Front Saloon succeeded in damaging two other saloons, two restaurants and a barbershop.

Congress had access to the railroad, some three miles away, by stage. When the Santa Fe, Prescott and Phoenix Railroad was extended south from Prescott, it was intended to reach Congress, but somehow missed the town by over three miles. Congress Junction was then maintained as the railroad station.

One day the stage pulled out of Congress with six passengers aboard. A few miles from the camp, two armed highwaymen masked with feed sacks pulled over their heads sprang into the path of the oncoming coach, demanding the driver to stop his team and all occupants to get out. As the travelers alighted from the stage, each was told to hand over his valuables; they obliged. The bandits, appearing satisfied with the possessions handed them, ordered the passengers back into the stage and quickly disappeared into the brush. These robbers were obviously amateurs. By not searching their victims they had deprived themselves of at least a thousand dollars more in money and personal belongings.

By 1905, Congress was supporting an active five hundred inhabitants. For thirty years more the towns lived, despite the gradual decrease in population. The Congress post office closed in 1938, and Congress Junction became known as Congress.

The ruins of old Congress are still visible. In "Mill Town" there are four buildings in various degrees of ruin. One roofless stone structure remains in "Lower Town." Situated between the two towns is a small cemetery.

Congress, 1898.—*Courtesy Arizona Pioneers' Historical Society*

Advertisement.—*Courtesy Arizona Pioneers' Historical Society*

"Diamond" Joseph Reynolds. ". . . Diamond Joe died in one of his houses (in Congress) February 21, 1891. The house splendidly furnished with the latest improvements; he also had the very best assistance as there is a good doctor employed by the company. After his death we had him packed in ice, and the coffin padded all around inside. No better attention could be given to anybody during sickness as five men were continually waiting on him, and all his wants were fully attended to."—*Arizona Enterprise*, April 4, 1891.—*Courtesy Sharlot Hall Museum*

Congress, May, 1900. Picture made the day President McKinley visited Congress.—*Courtesy Arizona Pioneers' Historical Society*

Congress, 1905, looking northeast.—*Courtesy Sharlot Hall Museum*

Congress, looking southwest from the mine site over the ruins, with Congress Junction in the background.

A grave in the Congress Cemetery, with the ruins of the mill in the background.

Constellation, *circa* 1912. Picture of the Monte Cristo Mine when Ezra W. Thayer tried to promote the property.—*Courtesy Sharlot Hall Museum*

40
C

Constellation. Monte Cristo Mine as it looks today.

Constellation

COUNTY: *Yavapai*
LOCATION: *11 mi. northeast of Wickenburg*
MAP: *pages 183-189*
P.O. est. as Constellation, April 29, 1901; discont. Jan. 31, 1939.

Constellation camp was situated at the site of the Monte Cristo Mine. Ezra W. Thayer, a Phoenix hardware merchant, promoted the mine from about 1912 to 1920. He never put the Monte Cristo into production, and eventually sold the property to an oil promoter. Although various mining companies were attempting to develop the gold wealth in the Constellation area as early as the turn of the century, the community did not seem to take root until sometime after 1920. By 1925, some 250 miners and other inhabitants sustained a post office, general store, and stage line.

Some of the mines worked were the Black Rock, Oro Grande, and Gold Bar.

Contention City

COUNTY: *Cochise*
LOCATION: *3 mi. north of Fairbank, east of the San Pedro River*
MAP: *page 195*
P.O. est. as Contention, April 6, 1880; discont. Nov. 26, 1888.

Three mills at Contention City—Grand Central, Head Center, and The Contention—reduced ore from the Tombstone mines and provided life for the milling community. Although it was a busy and important place, Contention City lived and died within one decade. When the Tombstone mines closed because of flooding, the mills ceased working.

Contention City, 1963. An aerial photograph showing one isolated ruin on the east side of the San Pedro River.—*Courtesy Historical Museum, Fort Huachuca*

Contention City was surveyed and laid out beside the San Pedro River in the latter part of 1879. In a few months the town, bustling with activity, claimed a population of over a hundred people, including ten American ladies who had arrived with their husbands. Two stage lines, Kinnear's and Ohnesorgen & Walker, brought passengers daily from Tucson and Tombstone. In business was John McDermott's saloon, the Western Hotel, a mercantile house, blacksmith shop, dairy, meat market, and Chinese laundry. Many other business concerns and professional men were quickly added to the growing "city," whose peak population probably did not exceed two hundred.

No impression has been left in fact or in fiction that Contention City was ever a very wild or tough town. No doubt there arose occasional disputes and threats. At one such time, a local altercation was settled by Major Clifton, who donned his authoritative judicial robes and held court in John McDermott's saloon.

Visitors to Contention City will find a few adobe walls and traces of a small cemetery.

Masons Western Hotel, Contention City, *circa* 1880.— *Courtesy Arizona Pioneers' Historical Society*

Contention City, *circa* 1880.—*Courtesy Arizona Pioneers' Historical Society*

Contention City, *circa* 1880. The Contention Mill—twenty-five stamps and thirty-five men—was one of three stamp mills that reduced the silver ore from the Tombstone mines.—*Courtesy Arizona Pioneers' Historical Society*

Copper Creek

COUNTY: *Pinal*
LOCATION: *10 mi. east of Mammoth*
MAP: *page 193*
P.O. est. as Copper Creek, March 6, 1907; discont. Aug. 31, 1942.

A winding, spectacular canyon road leads to the ruins of Copper Creek mining camp. Situated on the steep banks of Copper Creek in the Galiuro Mountains, the few remaining cement, rock, and wood foundations indicate that the town was built in tiers.

The community, started in the 1880's, soon matured into a busy, hardworking camp.

By 1910, three mining companies were operating in Copper Creek: Calumet & Arizona, Copper Creek, and Minnesota Arizona Mining. The town boasted some fifty buildings occupied by the two hundred miners and their families. A physician, a post office, Copper Creek Stage Line, and other concerns served the people.

Copper Creek. Concrete foundations and scattered lumber are all that is left of this mining camp.

Copper Hill

COUNTY: *Gila*
LOCATION: *3½ mi. northwest of Globe*
MAP: *page 191*
P.O. est. as Copper Hill, June 18, 1908; discont. Feb. 15, 1933.

Copper Hill grew into existence during the early 1900's as a camp for the Arizona Commercial, Iron Cap, and Superior and Boston mines. The prosperous community expanded to approximately five hundred people by 1925 and sufficient business enterprises followed this growth. In addition to the usual stores, boardinghouses, and offices found in most mining camps, Copper Hill was equipped with a hospital and a school.

The town's glory was short-lived. Five years later, only forty people remained. The Arizona Commercial Company was still doing some mining, but evidently not enough to keep the town going.

Mines, dumps, cement foundations, and scattered ruins along the canyon mark the site of Copper Hill.

Copper Hill. Ruins of a gravity feed mill in Copper Gulch, north of the site of Copper Hill.

43
c

Copper Hill, *circa* 1925. View of Copper Hill, from the scrapbook of Morris J. Elsing.—*Courtesy Arizona Pioneers' Historical Society*

Courtland

COUNTY: *Cochise*
LOCATION: *19 miles east of Tombstone*
MAP: *page 199*
P.O. est. as Courtland, March 13, 1909; discont. Sept. 30, 1942.

It is difficult to imagine Courtland's former prosperity by viewing what is left of the place today. Once a booming copper town with two thousand inhabitants, now Courtland is only the skeleton of a jail, two buildings, and a sole resident.

The arrival of four large mining companies (The Great Western, Calumet & Arizona, Copper Queen, and Leadville) heralded Courtland's boom in February, 1909. Within a few weeks, hundreds of people poured into the area, buildings mushroomed by the dozen, and every conceivable kind of business was established. Courtland boasted of the best. Such luxuries as fresh milk and bakery delivery services, an ice cream parlor, motion-picture theater, five miles of water mains, telephones, and a telegraph service became a daily part of the town's existence. Two newspapers quickly went into business. The El Paso & Southwestern and Southern Pacific Railroads rushed in to construct branch lines to the coming city.

Among the structures not immediately built in town was the jail. For a while a tunnel served the purpose. One event which took place here was an attempted jail break that backfired. A Mexican prisoner decided to burn his way to freedom. During the night, he placed his bedding against the tunnel door and set it afire. He assumed the door would burn, but, unfortunately for him, this did not occur. Instead, the smouldering bedding filled the tunnel with suffocating smoke, nearly terminating the prisoner's jail sentence. When Deputy Sheriff Bright arrived in the morning with breakfast for the Mexican, he found his charge unconscious. A good dose of fresh air revived him. Because of this incident and various other occurrences in the old tunnel, the new branch county jail was greatly appreciated by the Courtland officers.

Courtland's first year was marked by sundry events; the town's first wedding, a bit of cattle rustling, the end of a successful school term, and a horse race and baseball game on the Fourth of July.

Courtland lived for more than thirty years, although there were many ups and downs. Short bursts of activity and hope would follow slumps, but, after the first decade, Courtland was mostly on the decline. When the boom ended, buildings closed and people left. Other buildings were sold and moved away, but not everyone deserted Courtland. Enough people still lived there to keep the post office open until 1942.

Courtland—two remaining buildings.

Front page of the first edition of the *Courtland Arizonan.—Courtesy Arizona Pioneers' Historical Society*

COURTLAND ARIZONAN

"KEEP FAITH WITH THE PEOPLE AND THE PEOPLE WILL KEEP FAITH WITH YOU."

VOL. I. SATURDAY, FEBRUARY 13th, 1909. NO. 1.

HOME RULE FOR CITIES NOW LIKELY

PACE LOCAL OPTION BILL TO BE TAKEN UP BY THE ASSEMBLY ON MONDAY

MAJORITY OF BOTH HOUSES FAVORABLE TO AMENDMENT

Lobby Less Active Against the Bill Since Being Exposed in the Press of the Territory.

Phoenix, Feb. 13.—(Special to the Arizonan)—What will the legislature do with the Pace bill? That is what every liquor dealer and every temperance agitator in the territory would like to know. The bill comes out of the committee Monday and it is generally believed that it will be passed, but probably with an amendment giving the home rule privilege to all cities of the first class. It is probable this amendment will be fathered by Bailey in the assembly and Hampton in the council. In both houses a solid republican vote will line up for the original Pace bill, if its is forced to a vote, but at least three of the republicans are known to secretly favor the city home rule amendment.

When the motion was made on Wednesday last to allow the committee having the bill in hand until Monday to make its report, it went through by a vote of thirteen to eleven and the friends of the measure hailed the vote as a victory, but it must be remembered that Bailey voted to give the committee more time and it is almost certain the little democratic giant of Cochise is opposed to the measure as it stands.

Since the exposure in the columns of the Arizona press two weeks ago of the activities of the whiskey lobby composed of Bo. Whitesides, sergeant-at arms of the council and Callahan and Murray of Bisbee, both attaches of the house, and Frank Burns, the doorkeeper of that body, those gentlemen have attended strictly to their legislative jobs while in the capital building. The attitude of Kean St. Charles, the Mojave Councilman, who vehemently denounced the attempt of certain liquor interests of Kingman to influence his vote, and announced that he would vigorously support the bill, also set the liquor interests to thinking, and lobby activity suddenly ceased.

The majority of both houses is disposed to consider the Pace bill on the majority principle alone. But the liquor interests are still quite powerful in the cities of the territory, and ambitious members are loath to court the opposition of this element. One curious feature of the fight is that the better element of the saloon keepers in Arizona are disposed to take the Pace bill with the city home rule amendment. One of the best known liquor men in Phoenix made this statement today.

'The Model License league were right in the attitude they took at the recent national convention in Louisville. Whatever action is menacing the liquor business at the hands of the people now is due largely to the lawlessness of men engaged in our business. Selling liquor to minors, to habitual drunkards, keeping open back and side doors contrary to ordinance and an everlasting meddling in politics—these are the causes which have brought the prohibition agitation. The saloon men must wake up and recognize that knowledge is spreading as never before, that humanity in general is on its highest plane in the world's history and that our business must meet the better requirements the same as any other business. The profits are sufficient in well conducted places. Were such places the only ones, there would be no agitation today. All we have to do is to recognize conditions, clean up and stay clean. Then tris agitation will cease."

RECTOR TO RUN AGAIN

Washington, Feb. 13.—Jimmy Rector, the renowned sprinter from the University of Virginia, who competed at the Olympic games in London last summer, will compete in the George Washington indoor meet, which will be held in this city. Besides running on the Orange and Blue relay, Rector will compete in the 5 and 220 [illegible]

NEILL BAILEY,
Democratic Leader in the House and Father of the Direct Primary Bill.

GEORGIANS ARE TO LOCATE HERE:

NUMBER OF THE BEST FAMILIES IN THE CRACKER STATE FOR COURTLAND AND VICINITY

WILLIAM BRADFORD PLANS COURTLAND DRUG BUSINESS

Here on a Tour of Inspection, He Decides that Courtland and Southwest Are Big With Opportunities.

Edward Bradford, who for thirty years has been, with his brother, William Bradford, proprietor of the largest drug house in Polk county, in northern Georgia, has decided to locate in Courtland. Within a week he will probably have a building in course of erection, and within a month or six weeks will have in full operation one of the best equipped drug stores in the entire Southwest.

Mr. Bradford arrived in Bisbee less than two weeks ago as the emissary of a number of Georgia families, who wished to settle in a milder climate, on account of the health of certain members. A trip through the Sulphur Springs valley convinced Mr. Bradford of the wonderful possibilities of that section, and a number of the best families in northern Georgia will settle there within the next six months in consequence.

"This is certainly the land of opportunity," said Mr. Bradford with enthusiasm while in Courtland last Sunday. "I heard of the Sulphur Springs valley and Courtland through a letter written to my brother, William Bradford, in Cedartown, Georgia, some weeks ago. The letter aroused much interest, and I came out here as the agent of a number of families. The interest is not confined to our families, but extends to many others in Polk county. My report shall be quite optimistic both as regards Courtland and the beautiful valley running all the way from Pearce to Douglas. It is not a country for the penniless and shiftless, but from what I have seen, and from all I have learned through persistent inquiry, I am confident that money and energy will accomplish wonders in the valley.

"As to Courtland, no one can visit that hustling camp, and learn of its wonderful copper ledges, and not be impressed that it is a coming city. I shall probably invest considerable money in town nproperty and in a drug business there. Your climate is the finest I ever experienced in winter. The days are perfect, and I am told the summer climate of this section is ideal. It certainly looks good to me, and I am sure my people will vindicate my judgment."

PROTOCOL IS SIGNED TODAY

Washington, Feb. 13.—Special Commissioner Buchanan today telegraphed the state department that he had just signed a protocol with the Venezuelan government in settlement of the disputes between that country and the United States.

COURTLAND AS IT APPEARS TODAY

A CITY IN EMBRYO WITH ALL THE CRUDITIES OF THE FRONTIER AND HUSTLE OF MODERN METROPOLS

ABOUT 2,000 ALREADY IN THE FUTURE MINING CENTER

Tough Fighting Men of the Yellow Backs Safely Lacking and All Roam the Tented Streets Unarmed

The Courtland of today lies in a succession of canyons and little valleys opening into the Sulphur Springs Valley on the west aaout nine miles south of Pearce, thirty-five miles north of Bisbee and forty odd miles from Douglas.

Six weeks ago the present townsite was practically barren. Today in the neighborhood of 2,000 people are living in tents and shacks, by far the larger portion of whom are on the Courtland townsite opened three weeks ago by J. N. McFate just over the hill and across the division canyon known as no man's land west of the Great Western Mining company's townsite, which will surely be thrown open for purchase before the end of the present month.

The big stores of the new camp are at present located on land owned by the Great Western company but in the natural course of events these stores must be removed to other and permanent locations. They are at present situated over some of the richest workings of the Great Western company.

In the McFate Courtland townsite many are doing a lively business in all branches of trade. There are restaurants, groceries, general merchandise stores, a barber shop, pool room, hardware store and a number of "hotels" where one has the rare privilege, these formation days, of jumping at the chance to get a good bed over a dust floor for from seventy-five cents to a dollar and a half a night. The short order houses located in the various townsites are running to full capacity day and night.

Assurances have been given that within six months, or just as soon as the railroads are completed and ready to haul the ore to the Douglas smelters, from 1500 to 2000 men will be put to work in the shafts of the Great Western and Calumet and Arizona properties. Extensive development works in both properties have justified the statement published in another column that ore sufficient to produce 2,000,000 pounds of copper monthly for a period of four years has already been blocked out in the Great Western, Calumet and Arizona mines.

The present population of the town is scattered over an area a mile long. Hardly a building worthy of the name has been erected. Those of the Southwestern Mercantile company and the Renaud General Merchandise company are the best. Most of the buildings are board shacks, many half canvass and the majority just canvass tents.

Only a few of the 2,000 are in business. Most of the others are usual floaters of a prospective camp. Nearly all have money to invest in some business, but the chances for such investment will probably be much better two months from now.

There is not any over abundance of water and a bath is a real luxury. The town is distinctly orderly. There are only two saloons and one of these is some distance from either the McFate or the Great Western properties. The former commands a beautiful view of the Sulphur Springs valley to the north and east and the Great Western site overlooks the valley to the south.

Both the Southern Pacific and El Paso & Southwestern are pushing with might and main to get into the new camp. The Southern Pacific has a big grading force pushing south from Pearce. The road must enter Courtland through the McFate Courtland townsite and this fact, together with the natural location of that property, has given a big boom to realty there. Where the Southern Pacific depot will be located is not known for certain at present.

The El Paso & Southwestern is rushing work at both ends on the road which is to run between Courtland and Douglas. The depot site is in the Greatwestern townsite. Both railroads are rushing to get into the new camp within the next six months. All reports agree that eventually the Southern Pacific will push on to Douglas. Reports are rife that the extension to Douglas will be pushed without delay but officials of the company during the past week stated that for the present the company well make its terminal at Courtland.

COURTLAND TO BE AN OPEN TOWN

NONE OF THE BIG COMPANIES TO ENTER THE MERCANTILE BUSINESS IN THE NEW CAMP

PROSPECTIVE BUSINESS MEN MUCH PLEASED

Believe the New City Will Be a Man Makes Money and Fast

That none of the big mining companies upon whose development and prosperity the hope of Courtland rests are to establish a mercantile store of any kind whatever, is the announcement made by a mining official high in authority to an Arizonan representative Friday. The announcement has been hailed with satisfaction by many who have come to Courtland hoping that such a condition would prevail, and upon which depended the investment of thousands of independent capital in the new town.

While there is no feeling of hostility to the big corporations which have built the wonderful city of Bisbee, a feeling has prevailed for some time that it would be better for general mercantile conditions if the prospective independent merchants did not have to face the keen competition of the big stores in Courtland.

This decision on the part of the big companies means that every dollar of the pay rolls, which inside of a year will almost certainly amount to over $200,000 monthly, will find its way into general circulation, and an era of great prosperity result.

It is true that the Great Western Hardware company is mostly owned by certain gentlemen largely interested in the Great Western Mining company, but only as individuals, and the hardware company is in no sense a "company" proposition. Mercantile Courtland is to enjoy railway competition, assured by the rapid approachof the El Paso & Southwestern and the Southern Pacific towards the new town.

CUTTING KNOX DOWN TO FIT NEW OFFICE

Washington, Feb. 13.—By a vote of 5 to 3 the house committee on election of president vice president and representatives today agreed on a favorable report of the bill to reduce the salary of the secretary of state, making Senator Knox eligible for that office. A minority report is to be presented.

ORE IN SIGHT TO KEEP THE RAILROADS BUSY FOR FOUR YEARS, SAYS OFFICIAL

Great Western and Calumet And Arizona Claims In the Courtland District, Ready To Begin Producing, 2,000,000 Pounds Per Month

NO OTHER CAMP IN ARIZONA EVER NADE SUCH A SHOWING IN SO SHORT A TIME

Astonishing Statement by a High Official of One of the Big Copper Companies Leaves No Doubt of the Permanency of the Coming Metropolis

That the development work in the Germania shaft of the Calumet & Arizona, and by the Great Western company is responsible for the feverish haste with which the Southern Pacific is building south and the El Paso & Southwestern north from Douglas into the new camp, is not to be questioned. It was learned Friday from an official of the Great Western company that sufficient ore has been blocked out to produce from the Germania and Great Western shafts 2,000,000 pounds of copper monthly for the next four years.

"There has never been another camp in the history of Arizona which has developed so great a tonnage of as high grade ore in the same length of time," said the official quoted. "Since the station was cut on the Germania and Great Western on August 1 last, over 8,000 feet of development work has been done, better than 90 per cent of which runs through ore running seven and one-half per cent or over. This is a conservative estimate. In fact, during this time enough has been demonstrated in these workings to interest two well known railroads to the extent of vieing with each other in reaching the new camp, and in the least possible time.

"At present there are four companies operating here, the Great Western, Calumet & Arizona, Copper Queen and Leadville. The Calumet & Arizona, of which Colonel L. W. Powell is the vice president and general manager, and John S. Talbot superintendent, own twentyseven claims lying in a group. The Great Western company owns a group of seventeen patented claims, patented by the Young brothers, of Clinton, Iowa. Colonel Talbot is the superintendent for this company. The Copper Queen has a group of nineteen claims, and the Leadville company twenty-one.

"There is ore enough in sight in the Great Western and the Germania shafts to guarantee sufficient tonnage of seven and one-half per cent ore to produce 2,000,000 pounds of ore monthly for the next four years. The Germania No. 1 shaft is down 317 feet; over 7,000 feet of tunneling, raising and winzeing has been done, connecting with the Mary shaft of the Great Western, proving the continuity of the ore bodies from one to the other. The Mary shaft of the Great Western is 200 feet deep, with over 3,000 feet of drifting, raising and winzeing. The combined work in these two shafts show that ninety per cent or better of the entire workings are in big bodies of ore of the seven and a half per cent grade.

"Within the next six months there should be between 1,500 and 2,000 men working in the mines of the two companies already developed."

The Leadville and Copper Queen people are doing development work along the lines begun by the Great Western and Calumet & Arizona last August. The outlook is more than promising. Big ore bodies, it is declared, have been tapped, and if reports are to be credited, the Copper Queen and Leadville will soon be dupicating th records of the other two companies made in the past six months.

KIBBEY'S VETOES LIKELY TO RAISE BIG STORM IN COUNCIL

Weedin, of Pinal, Expected to Take Advantage of an Opportunity to Pay Off An Old Political Grudge on the Governor

Courtland Arizonan Bureau,
Phoenix, Arizona, February 13.

That Governor Kibbey will on Monday or Tuesday sent in his veto of the Weedin bills abolishing the offices of public examiner and the rangers, is the expectation of the politicians at the territorial capital at this writing. That the veto will cause a bitter denunciation of Governor Kbbey at the hands of the author of the bills is also confidently expected, for the fighting member from Pinal has not caused his intention to be hidden in the slightest degree.

Weedin's friends are telling it around the capital that his real purpose in introducing the ranger and pubic examiner bills was to giive him an oppor tunty of attackng the governor, who, Wedin knew would certainly veto both bills. Weedin, it is declared, has ready to deliver a carefully prepared typewritten speech, rehashing in detail the record of the governor while the latter was acting as federal judge in Pinal, Gila and Graham counties during Grover Cleveland's second term. It is no secret in official circles in Arizona that Judge Kibbey was removed by wire by Cleveland while holding a court session at Globe, and the real reasons therefore have been typewritten in detail by Weedin for delivery when he rises to a question of privilege following the motion to pass the ranger bill over the governor's veto.

Weedin will go into details regarding the obliteration of the court records at Florence, which form part of the charges which have been filed in Washington in opposition to Governor Kibbey's confirmation by the senate. Weedin in his speech to the council following the motion to override the governor's veto, will declare that after Francis J. Heney had been rebuked by Judge Kibbey and fined for playing cards with a number of jurymen on the night of the first day's trial of a notorious adultery case, Heney discovered that while he was playing hearts with the jurymen, the judge was engaged in eating tamales with the fair defendant in the case. Thereupon, Weedin will declare, Governor Kibbey was bitterly assailed by Heney for his inconsistency, coupled with threats of what was likely to happen in case Heney's fine was not rescinded and the court record expunged.

Weedin will go further and give in detail an account of a humorous incident in the governor's life in which an almond-eyed celestial of Florence and a laundry bill largely figured. The incident will probably be recalled by scores of Arizona lawyers who were in

(Continue to page five.)

Courtland, 1910. At the time of this picture Courtland had a population of about 2,000. (1) Company Boarding House, (2) Engineers Office, (3) General Managers Office, (4) Germania Shaft, (5) April Fool Shaft, (6) Miami Shaft.—*Courtesy Arizona Pioneers' Historical Society*

46
c

Advertisements from the *Courtland Arizonan.—Courtesy Arizona Pioneers' Historical Society*

Courtland, 1909. Out for a ride in a new Stevens-Duryee. —*Courtesy Arizona Pioneers' Historical Society*

SENDING FOR MEAT

is as safe as calling in person, when it's this meat market that is being patronized, one trial convinces,

A CHILD BUYS MEAT

here with absolute assurance of fair treatment. Whoever you may send will bring back what you want. For confidence and safety buy here.

THE COURTLAND MEAT CO.

GOOD LIVING

CARTER & WOOD

BEST SHORT ORDER HOUSE IN COURTLAND. CHOICEST CUTS OF STEAKS, CROPS AND CUTLETS AT POPULAR PRICES.

COURTLAND, ...ARIZONA.

Looking north along the main street of Courtland, with the jail in the foreground.

Crown King

COUNTY: *Yavapai*
LOCATION: *31 mi. south of Prescott*
MAP: *page 189*
P.O. est. as Crown King, June 29, 1888; discont. May 15, 1954.

The famous Crown King (Crowned King) gold mine is situated near the center of the Bradshaw Mountains. The mine, first discovered in the early 1870's, came to life during the Bradshaw excitement. It was called the Red Rock and later the Buckeye. After the property came into possession of N. C. Sheckles and Company, the name became Crown King.

Crown King settlement began taking form in the 1880's. The camp was quiet, clean, and orderly. The company did not tolerate drunkenness in their employees, therefore, a more respectable type of man was attracted to the camp. The miners were industrious, intelligent, and fond of reading. Only the hangers-on indulged in heavy drinking and gambling.

By 1897 the town contained the usual company stores, several saloons, boardinghouses, two Chinese restaurants and a feed yard. More unusual in this remote mountain village was the presence of electricity and one telephone.

At first the Crown King Company employed a pack train to carry the rich ore and concentrates forty miles to Prescott, at a cost of $21.50 a ton. Completion of the Crown King branch line of the Prescott and Eastern Railroad in 1904 fortunately changed this procedure. The railroad also served as an incentive for more merchants and other residents to populate the region.

In 1901 the Crown King Mine became involved in litigation and was closed for a number of years. Other working mines in the Bradshaws managed to keep the community of Crown King prospering.

A few year-round residents and summer vacationers still reside at Crown King.

Prospector's palace, *circa* 1907.—*Courtesy Sharlot Hall Museum*

Crown King, *circa* 1885. Inside the boiler room at the Crown King Mine. Steam was generated to operate machinery in the mill.—*Courtesy Sharlot Hall Museum*

Shift at the Crown King Mine, *circa* 1885.—*Courtesy Sharlot Hall Museum*

DeNoon

COUNTY: *Pinal*
LOCATION: *about 13 m. southwest of Superior*
MAP: *page 191*
P.O. est. as DeNoon, March 19, 1890; discont. April 1, 1891.

There seems to be some question as to whether DeNoon was the milling or the mining town for the Reymert Mine. It was probably the milling town.

James DeNoon Reymert was responsible for the founding and naming of the camp. Born in Norway in 1821, Reymert came to America in 1842. He lived in Wisconsin, New York, and Chile before settling in Arizona Territory about 1876. Reymert opened a law office, edited the *Pinal Drill*

newspaper, and organized the Reymert silver mine in Pinal County.

DeNoon was located some two miles from the Reymert Mine. As an embryo camp in 1889 it was growing rapidly, and consequently anticipated great importance within a short time. A well-stocked general store, two saloons and 150 men and families formed the town. Plans for the building of a large hotel were imminent, but probably never became an actuality.

Obviously, DeNoon did not attain paramount status. The post office was only able to survive one year, and it is doubtful that the camp lived much longer.

Dos Cabezas

COUNTY: *Cochise*

LOCATION: *14 mi. southeast of Willcox on Arizona 186*

MAP: *page 199*

P.O. est. as Dos Cabezas, April 8, 1879; discont. Jan. 31, 1960.

Dos Cabezas, a sleepy little village of adobe ruins and deserted dwellings—home to a few people—was first settled in 1878 as a result of gold and silver mines nearby. By the mid 1880's three stamp mills, a brewery, brickyard, district school, hotel, blacksmith shop, barber shop, general store, and about three hundred people comprised Dos Cabezas.

Two brothers named Casey were doing some prospecting in the Dos Cabezas region. After staking a claim on the mountain slope, they proceeded to construct a shelter near their mine. Although it was only a crude dugout, it became their home and "castle." The Casey brothers' mine proved to be quite rich. As word about their valuable property circulated, many eager parties sought to purchase the land from them. Finally a Tombstone attorney and his associates persuaded the brothers to agree to sell for forty thousand dollars. Later, when the attorney returned to close the deal, he found that the Caseys had decided not to sell. Thoroughly mystified by their sudden change of mind, the Tombstone gentleman kindly tried to explain to the brothers that selling out to men who had the capital to develop the mine would mean employment and business for the people of Dos Cabezas. Also, he informed them that the forty thousand dollars they would receive was more money than they ever could obtain by working the mine themselves. The Caseys agreed all was true, but did not the lawyer understand that their dugout home was on the mine property? If they sold, where would they live!

Dos Cabezas maintained a fairly consistent level of prosperity well into the twentieth century. Then, as mines failed to produce, the community slipped into its present condition.

Dos Cabezas, 1901. Virginia Milling Co. in the Dos Cabezas Mountains.—*Courtesy Arizona Pioneers' Historical Society*

Adobe ruins at Dos Cabezas.

Deserted building at present-day Dos Cabezas.

Ehrenberg

COUNTY: *Yuma*
LOCATION: *2 mi. north of present-day Ehren-berg*
MAP: *page 177*
P.O. est. as Ehrenberg, Sept. 20, 1869; discont. Dec. 31, 1913.

Ehrenberg—this cemetery is located about half a mile north of present-day Ehrenberg.

In the 1870's, when the Colorado River served as a main source of transportation to interior points of Arizona Territory, Ehrenberg was a major port.

Laid out in 1863 by an association of which Herman Ehrenberg was surveyor, the town was first named Mineral City. The place did not amount to much under this appellation. A clustering of tents, crude huts, and sixteen male inhabitants made up the "city." In 1867, the townsite was resurveyed and officially established as Ehrenberg, in honor of Herman Ehrenberg, the German pioneer surveyor and engineer. Ehrenberg never knew of the town which bore his name. The year before, he had been murdered at Dos Palmas, California.

During the exodus from La Paz about 1870 (six miles north of Ehrenberg), Ehrenberg acquired people and importance. The 1870 census records show a growth of eighty-seven dwellings and ninety-six families. From this time on, Ehrenberg gained prominence, not only as the principal shipping point on the river, but also as one of the most prosperous towns in the territory. Leading mercantile firms in Ehrenberg bore the names of J. Goldwater & Bro., J. M. Barney, and J. M. Castenado.

By 1872 a public school had been established, with Mary Elizabeth Post as teacher. The schoolroom, quite unusual in comparison to our present-day standards, was a former saloon with a roof supported by a series of arches which were closed at night by wooden doors. The earth floor was diligently sprinkled and swept every morning. When the teacher from the east, Miss Post, arrived in Ehrenberg, no doubt she felt like a foreigner in her new surroundings. All her pupils were Spanish-speaking, and she knew not a word of the language. Fortunately, a school trustee who spoke both English and Spanish came to her aid.

By the mid-1870's Ehrenberg was booming. The population had grown to five hundred. Besides stores, saloons, corrals, and a blacksmith and wagon shop, there were two bakeries, a hotel, a Catholic church, and the stage offices of the California and Arizona Stage Company.

Jesus Daniel was appointed to the important but unglamorous office of postmaster in 1884. Daniel must have appeared somewhat miscast in this docile role. Having lost an arm, he always wore a gun belt and a side arm. Furthermore, his enthusiasm for prospecting apparently left little time for his postal duties. When Post Office Inspector Waterbury arrived unexpectedly, he found over 150 undelivered letters. There were some 54 unopened official letters from Washington. One of these was from Postmaster General John Wannamaker, praising Daniel for his efficiency in conducting the affairs of the office.

Ehrenberg went into a serious decline in the early 1900's. The populace departed, leaving behind their adobe and tin buildings. Soon the elements and vandals had reduced this once flourishing settlement to negligible ruins.

A monument was erected in the old Ehrenberg cemetery in 1935 by the Arizona State Highway Department. As a fitting memorial to Arizona pioneers, relics of the past were cemented into an apron surrounding the base of the rock and mortar obelisk.

Colorado River steamer, date unknown.—*Courtesy Arizona Pioneers' Historical Society*

Advertisement from Richard J. Hinton, *The Handbook to Arizona*. San Francisco, Payot, Upham & Co., 1878.

Arizona Travelers, Attention!

J. GOLDWATER & BRO.

EHRENBERG and PRESCOTT,

Established in the Territory for over sixteen years. Do a General Wholesale and Retail Merchandise Business. Particular attention paid to

THE FORWARDING OF GOODS AND BAGGAGE

To any part of the Territory when consigned to our care.

TRAVELERS, TOURISTS, PROSPECTORS and OTHERS
WILL FIND

Our Stores supplied with everything needed to meet the wants of the country.

Checks on all parts of the United States Cashed, and Drafts Drawn on all parts of California and Arizona.

Fairbank station on the Southern Pacific Railroad.

Fairbank

COUNTY: *Cochise*
LOCATION: *10 mi. west of Tombstone on Arizona 82*
MAP: *page 195*
P.O. est. as Fairbank, May 16, 1883.

The community was named for N. K. Fairbank, a Chicago merchant, who organized the Grand Central Mining Company in Tombstone. Settled around 1882, Fairbank served as an important railroad supply point and a stage terminal for mail and express. Long before that time, in the 1700's, it was the site of an Indian village called Santa Cruz.

The town contained a steam quartz mill, Wells Fargo & Company office, a meat market, grocery, general store, restaurants, saloons and a hundred or more people.

In February, 1900, the notorious Billy Stiles–Burt Alvord gang attempted a robbery in Fairbank. Accompanying the two infamous leaders were the Owen brothers, a man named Brown, Bravo Horn, and a particularly bad desperado, Three-Fingered Jack Dunlap. Their objective was to rob the Wells Fargo box from the express car of the train when it stopped at the Fairbank station to take on passengers. The plan seemed simple, except for the fact that celebrated lawman Jeff Milton was guarding the payroll inside the express car. When Milton refused to hand over the treasure, the men opened fire. In the short volley that followed, Three-Fingered Jack was injured and Milton's arm was badly shattered. Realizing he was losing a lot of blood and that he might lose consciousness, Milton quickly opened the opposite door of the Wells Fargo express car and threw out the key to the payroll box.

By this time the gunshots had attracted attention. As the excited townspeople gathered, the gang was forced to abandon the attempted robbery. Quickly lashing their injured fellow gunman, Three-Fingered Jack, to a horse, they made a hasty retreat. The next day Jack Dunlap was found by a posse about nine miles from Fairbank, where he had been deserted by his companions. He lived only long enough to make a confession.

Meanwhile, Jeff Milton was rushed to a hospital in San Francisco. When told that his injured arm would have to be amputated, Milton loudly protested that if his arm were amputated he would kill the man who did it. Needless to say, Milton's arm was not removed, and he later recovered partial use of it.

Today Fairbank is a quiet little railroad town with a country store and post office.

Fairbank, *circa 1890.—Courtesy Arizona Pioneers' Historical Society*

Burt Alvord—law officer turned bad man—a highly respected constable at Willcox who became one of the best-known western train robbers of his era.—*Courtesy Arizona Pioneers' Historical Society*

Billy Stiles, law officer turned train robber. After Stiles agreed to be a witness at Burt Alvord's trial, he raided the Tombstone jail before the trial started and freed Alvord.—*Courtesy Arizona Pioneers' Historical Society*

Early railroad depot at Fairbank.—*Courtesy Arizona Pioneers' Historical Society*

Present-day Fairbank.

Fortuna

COUNTY: *Yuma*
LOCATION: *about 45 mi. southeast of Yuma in the Gila Mountains*
MAP: *page 181*
P.O. *est. as Fortuna, Sept. 30, 1896; discont. Nov. 30, 1904.*

La Fortuna Mine lies close to the *Camino del Diablo*, a route that gained notoriety from the appalling number of deaths along this hazardous 150-mile stretch of desert. The loss of lives grew to staggering proportions in 1849, as inadequately-equipped gold rush parties attempted to traverse the desolate, waterless region and perished from thirst. Again in 1860, placer gold discovered in the Colorado River valley sent another wave of travelers, mostly Mexicans, along the hellish highway to their deaths. Appropriately called the Road of Death, the *Camino del Diablo,* soon dotted with crudely-marked stone graves, was almost entirely abandoned as being too dangerous.

The region was not completely worthless, since it did produce La Fortuna gold mine. For years, many prospectors had completely overlooked the gold outcrop while passing along the *Camino del Diablo*. Not until December 22, 1894, was the ledge discovered and a claim staked. First located by Charles W. Thomas, Laurent Albert, and William H. Holbert, the mine was sold to Charles D. Lane of Angels Camp, California, in 1896. Lane organized La Fortuna Gold Mining and Milling Company. Scarcity of water was obviously a major problem. A large, 100-horsepower pump placed at the Gila River and a pipeline laid to the mine remedied the situation. The company also built a twenty-stamp mill at the mine and employed eighty to a hundred men.

The adobes, tents, and improvised dwellings of one sort or another clustered irregularly around the mill became known as Fortuna. Good meals were furnished at the hotel, saloons provided substitutes for the saline taste of the water, and a stage and freight line connected Fortuna with Blaisdell, a station on the Southern Pacific Railroad.

La Fortuna Company operated actively until 1904, and intermittent work continued for about the next twenty years.

No buildings remain at the site of Fortuna.

Freight wagons. The team of mules hitched to these freighters could move 12,000 to 18,000 pounds across the Arizona desert.—*Courtesy Arizona Pioneers' Historical Society*

Frisco, *circa* 1910. Ball mill crusher on way to the Frisco Mill.—*Courtesy Mohave Pioneers Historical Society*

Frisco

COUNTY: *Mohave*
LOCATION: *about 25 mi. west of Kingman*
MAP: *page 175*
P.O. est. as Frisco, May 5, 1913; discont. July 15, 1915.

Frisco gold mine was located about 1894, and later the camp of Frisco was established. The mine ore deposit dipped beneath the town, and only a capping of rhyolite prevented Frisco from having streets of gold. The camp contained no saloons, just a well-stocked store, post office, boarding house and a few other businesses. Frisco, a peaceful town, claimed about 150 residents. Many of the miners were married and lived in comfortable adobe houses.

Team hauling engine components from the camp to the Frisco Mine, *circa* 1910.—*Courtesy Mohave Pioneers Historical Society*

Frisco, *circa* 1910. The first large diesel engine in Mohave County, a BeLavern, at the Frisco Mine.—*Courtesy Mohave Pioneers Historical Society*

Galeyville

COUNTY: *Cochise*
LOCATION: *6 mi. northwest of Portal*
MAP: *page 199*
P.O. est. as Galeyville, Jan. 6, 1881; discont. May 31, 1882.

In 1880, John H. Galey, an oil man from Pennsylvania, was attracted to the Chiricahua Mountains by the high price of silver. He bought a silver claim, opened the Texas Mine, built a smelter, organized the Texas Mining and Smelting Company, and founded the boom camp of Galeyville.

Although the town died a sudden death after barely two years, Galeyville left an indelible impression as a refuge and hangout for outlaws and cattle rustlers. A party of rustlers would ride into Mexico, steal cattle, and bring them across the border at a point near Galeyville. Here the stolen stock would be divided, branded, and eventually sold to Arizona ranchers. Most noted and remembered of the rustlers were Curly Bill Brocius and Johnny Ringo.

William Brocius acquired his nickname because of his dark, kinky hair. Tall, rugged, and blue-eyed, Curly Bill wore a wide-brimmed sombrero, fancy-stitched boots, and two criss-crossed gun belts for his twin forty-fours. Well liked and respected by many men, Curly Bill was even willing to give the law a hand. Once Deputy Sheriff William Breckenridge asked Bill if he would be willing to go with him as deputy assessor and help collect taxes from the rustlers. Although amused, Brocius eagerly accepted, and the next day the two started out. Curly Bill led Breckenridge into many of the dead-end canyons and hiding places where the rustlers had their stolen cattle. After introducing Breckenridge to his fellow thieves, Brocius made sure that they all payed their taxes.

Curly Bill almost met a premature death at Galeyville in 1881. Jim Wallace, angered at Brocius during a drinking bout, staggered outside the saloon, got a rifle, and shot Bill. The bullet hit the left side of his neck just below the ear and exited below the right jaw. It was a miracle that Brocius was not immediately killed. For a while no one thought he would live, but he did.

How and when Curly Bill's life ended is still somewhat of a mystery. He was reportedly killed by Wyatt Earp at Iron Springs, but then he was seen a short time after his supposed death. Old-timers say he visited Tombstone in the 1920's. Bill's fellow cattle rustler, Johnny Ringo, committed suicide on July 14, 1882.

Galeyville was not made up exclusively of rustlers and outlaws. There were many hard-working miners and merchants. About four hundred people formed the town's population. Galeyville reported having eleven saloons, six merchandise stores, two hotels, two restaurants, two butcher shops, two blacksmith and wagon shops, three lumberyards, a dairy, a jeweler, lawyers, a notary public, an assayer, a justice of the peace, physicians, a shoemaker, a Wells Fargo office, and a short-lived newspaper.

John Galey had started out with high hopes of accumulating a fortune in silver, but his dreams were never realized. When he left Galeyville he was badly in debt. After receiving threatening letters from his creditors, Galey borrowed money, returned to Galeyville, and satisfied all debts. The mine closed, the smelter moved to Benson, and Galeyville emptied as rapidly as it had filled. Since most of the buildings were made of wood, they were later torn down and the lumber carted off to the nearby town of Paradise.

Galeyville—all that remains at Galeyville is this sign.

GALEYVILLE

ESTABLISHED 1881   POPULATION 400

JOHN H. GALEY OPENED THE TEXAS MINE AND SMELTER IN 1881. MINING BOOMED AND DIED AND THE TOWN BECAME A HAVEN FOR LAWLESS MEN LIKE CURLY BILL AND JOHN RINGO WHO USED NEARBY GULCHES TO HOLD STOLEN CATTLE WHILE BRANDS WERE ALTERED.   IN 1888 THE SAN SIMON CATTLE COMPANY FORCED OUT SQUATTERS AND THE REMAINS OF GALEYVILLE WERE CARRIED AWAY TO CONSTRUCT HOUSES IN NEARBY PARADISE. . . . .

John H. Galey (1840–1918), early developer of the Titusville, Pennsylvania, oil boom and financier and promoter of the silver mines around Galeyville.—*Courtesy Arizona Pioneers' Historical Society*

Germa

COUNTY: *Mohave*
LOCATION: *2 mi. southwest of Oatman*
MAP: *page 175*
P.O. est. as Germa, Jan. 20, 1903; discont. Feb. 27, 1906.

In 1896 a gold deposit was discovered just west of Vivian (Oatman). Four years later the property came into the hands of the German-American Mining Company. Both the mine and the small community supported by the mine became known as Germa. An insufficient water supply to run the mill on a double shift closed the Germa Mine in 1906. As a result, Germa camp died. A few foundations still mark the site.

Garces

COUNTY: *Cochise*
LOCATION: *about 10 mi. south of Sierra Vista*
MAP: *page 195*
P.O. est. as Reef, Jan. 7, 1901; changed to Palmerlee, Dec. 7, 1904; changed to Garces, April 12, 1911; discont. May 24, 1926.

The now-vanished mining camp of Garces functioned in earlier years under the names of Reef and Palmerlee. When a post office was first established there in 1901, the community was given the name of Reef, for the Reef Mine. A few years later the name changed to Palmerlee, for Joseph S. Palmerlee, the postmaster and owner of a general store in the camp. Palmerlee reported having a hundred inhabitants, a florist, meat market, second-hand merchandise shop, boardinghouse, school, and other concerns. Eventually the community acquired the name of Garces, by which it was known for the remaining fifteen years of its life. Garces supported up to two hundred people.

Germa, *Circa* 1906. The Germa Mine produced about $40,000 worth of gold.—*Courtesy U.S. Geological Survey*

Gila City

COUNTY: *Yuma*
LOCATION: *20 mi. east of Yuma*
MAP: *page 181*
P.O. est. as Gila City, Dec. 24, 1858; discont.
    July 14, 1863.

Rich placer gold was discovered by Jacob Snively along the Gila River in early 1858. As news of Arizona's golden wealth leaked out, hundreds rushed from California and elsewhere to make an easy fortune. In no time at all, Gila City sprang up on the riverbank and mushroomed into a booming camp of tents, shanties and adobe houses. The town boasted some twelve hundred residents and about everything else except a jail and a church. The gold furor was running high. Some men were mining $30.00 to $125.00 worth of gold a day; others could afford to pay miners $3.00 a day plus their board to work the lower-grade deposits. The gulches and banks of the Gila were turned inside out for the precious metal, and even the crudest equipment and least-skilled hands were employed. Just when Gila City's merchants and miners seemed to be prospering, the rich pay dirt gave out. The population diminished as miners moved to La Paz, on the Colorado River, where gold had been discovered in 1862. That same year a flood nearly obliterated withering Gila City. By the mid-1860's the only visible remains of the boom city were three chimneys.

Gillett

COUNTY: *Yavapai*
LOCATIONS *40 mi. north of Phoenix west of
    Interstate 17*
MAP: *page 189*
P.O. est. at Gillett, Oct. 15, 1878; discont. Aug.
    11, 1887.

Once an active milling town for the Tip Top silver mine, Gillett now consists of adobe and rock ruins. The community was founded on the Agua Fria River and named for Dan B. Gillett, the Tip Top Mine superintendent.

Gillett was a lively place. The mill pounded away profitably, and the miners quenched their thirst in the town's several saloons. Various stores (one opened by Charles T. Hayden, father of Arizona's senator, Carl Hayden) and other businesses served the people.

The town's blacksmith earned a larger income than his trade justified. This was due to a secondary occupation. Several times the blacksmith successfully managed to hold up the Wells Fargo stagecoach in Squaw Creek Canyon. By the time the stage arrived in Gillett the blacksmith would be back in his shop, busily occupied by his trade. One day a detective sent to investigate the hold-ups was observing a poker game in one of Gillett's saloons. Evidently the blacksmith was losing heavily. Excusing himself, the smithy left the saloon and returned minutes later with a pile of gold coins, which he plunked down and proceeded to gamble away. The hawk-eyed detective, noting that the coins were covered with mud, immediately became suspicious. A search of the blacksmith shop and a confession by the frightened smithy revealed the stolen gold coins cached in the bottom of a quenching tub.

On June 12, 1878, two killings and a lynching took place in Gillett within a few hours. A man named Setwright became involved in an argument in a saloon, and broke a bottle over the head of his adversary. Sheriff James C. Burnett stepped inside and arrested Setwright for his drunken behavior. Later in the day, Mr. Weir, a respected citizen, asked the sheriff to release Setwright into his custody so that he could take the drunk to his camp and sober him up. Burnett agreed, and the two set off for Weir's camp. A short time later, the mule Weir had been riding wandered back into Gillett. An immediate investigation produced Weir's body, shot through the head, some two hundred yards up the trail. Sheriff Burnett and several other men saddled their horses and took off in search of Setwright. A mile and a half from Gillett, near Moore's Station, he was captured. The prisoner was taken back to Gillett and placed inside a house in the custody of the sheriff, Colonel Taylor, and E. P. Raines.

By now, word had spread of the recent murder, and an angry mob of citizens began collecting outside the building where Setwright was being held. As time passed, the crowd became more frenzied and more bent on dealing out their own kind of punishment. Burnett tried to calm the mob by telling them that Setwright would be taken to Prescott, where law and justice would decide his fate.

The demands and threats of the excited throng only increased. Unless Setwright was delivered to them, they would blow up or burn down the building. Colonel Taylor stepped outside with his double-barreled shotgun, in an attempt to stop the crowd. Someone aimed a gun, a shot followed, and Taylor slumped to the ground, dead. Realizing it was impossible to defend their prisoner from the bloodthirsty citizens, Burnett and Raines released him. The now terrified and sober Setwright was dragged from the house, and minutes later his body was swinging from the limb of a cottonwood tree.

Gillett. Ruins of the Burfind Hotel, all that is left of the once active milling town.

Dan B. Gillett, *circa* 1878, superintendent of the Tip Top Mine, after whom the mill town of Gillett was named. — *Courtesy Arizona Pioneers' Historical Society*

61
G

Gleeson

COUNTY: *Cochise*

LOCATION: *16 mi. east of Tombstone*

MAP: *page 195*

P.O. est. as Turquoise, Oct. 22, 1890; discont. Sept. 17, 1894. Re-est. as Gleeson, Oct. 15, 1900; discont. March 31, 1939.

Gleeson was established near the site of an older mining camp known as Turquoise. Long before white men penetrated the region looking for mineralization, turquoise deposits were being mined by the Indians. During the 1870's, white men discovered copper, lead, and silver in the area. As claims were located and worked, the camp of Turquoise developed.

Turquoise flourished into the mid-1890's and probably was a typical mining camp of rugged miners and saloons. A noteworthy side light is that San Francisco millionaire George Hearst visited the mines at Turquoise in 1882.

John Gleeson (born in Ireland, 1861) and his wife came to Arizona in the 1890's. They settled in Pearce, where Gleeson worked as a miner. He must have done a little prospecting on his own, for in 1896 he discovered the Leonard, or Copper Belle, deposit on an older mining claim near Turquoise. Development of the Leonard proved it to be a valuable copper producer. About the turn of the century, Turquoise camp was moved to a lower site in order to obtain a more adequate water supply and was then renamed for John Gleeson.

The new camp was slow in getting started. Not until 1909 did the small community mature into a town of five hundred people.

A devastating fire destroyed much of Gleeson in June, 1912. Bucket brigades helped save a few buildings, but because of the poor fire-fighting facilities, twenty-eight buildings burned to the ground. Undaunted, the town rebuilt and continued to thrive. World War I and the demand for copper helped to boost Gleeson's economy and growth.

As the years passed, Gleeson gradually began to shrivel into a has-been mining town. By 1940, Gleeson had lost its post office and most of its occupants. Today a few residents and several deserted ruins occupy the site.

Mining hospital at Gleeson, date unknown. — *Courtesy Arizona Pioneers' Historical Society*

Gleeson—ruins of the general store on Gleeson's main street.

Gleeson, date un-
known. Burros and
sacked ore waiting
for the trip to the
mill.—*Courtesy
Sharlot Hall Museum*

Golconda

COUNTY: *Mohave*
LOCATION: *about 15 mi. north of Kingman*
MAP: *page 175*
P.O. est. as Golconda, Dec. 8, 1909; discont. Feb. 28, 1918.

Situated in the Cerbat range, Golconda Mine was discovered in the 1860's and worked for gold. In the early years of its production, ore from the mine was crushed in an arrastra and sold to local custom mills. After John Boyle acquired the mine sometime during the first decade of the present century, Golconda camp formed. The town was large enough to support a store, poolroom, school, and a justice of the peace.

In October, 1917, oil in one of the mill's flotation tanks boiled over, ignited, and started a terrific fire. All the men were put to work fighting the flames, but to no avail. Rapidly the fierce blaze reduced the mill to a charred skeleton. Although the cookhouse, poolroom, and a few other buildings in close proximity to the mill were destroyed, a lucky shift in the prevailing wind spared others.

A drop in the price of lead and zinc at about the same time as the fire occurred closed the mine. The mill was never rebuilt, and the mining community of Golconda soon ceased to exist. One building, a mill tailings pile, and a few foundations mark the site of the former town.

Looking west over the mining camp of Golconda, before 1918.—*Courtesy Thomas Mc-Michael*

Adit of a typical operating mine in the vicinity of Golconda. The ventilation piping on the right and the compressed air lines on the left provide these necessities to the working areas within the mine.

Golconda—abandoned ore car on a waste dump.

Gold Basin

COUNTY: *Mohave*
LOCATION: *about 50 mi. north of Kingman*
MAP: *page 175*
P.O. est. as Gold Basin, Sept. 20, 1890; discont. Jan. 4, 1894. Re-est. as Basin, March 17, 1904; discont. June 15, 1907.

Mining in the Gold Basin district had commenced by the 1870's. Although a five-stamp mill was erected to process the high-grade ore, general remoteness and scarcity of fuel and water restricted operations. The nearest source of water was the Colorado River, some thirty miles away. Plans were made to construct a narrow-gauge road from the mines to the river in hopes of making Gold Basin one of the most productive camps in the territory.

The community of Gold Basin was probably never very large. A post office to serve the miners functioned for a few years in the 1890's. Renewed activity about 1904 reopened the post office under the name of Basin. Some of the mines worked at that time were the Golden Slipper, Josephine, and Southern Bride.

Goldfield

COUNTY: *Pinal*
LOCATION: *6 mi. northeast of Apache Junction*
MAP: *page 191*
P.O. est. as Goldfield, Oct. 7, 1893; discont. Nov. 2, 1898. Re-est. as Youngsberg, June 8, 1921; discont. Oct. 30, 1926.

Goldfield was produced by a large but low-grade gold deposit discovered about 1892 on the western slope of the Superstition Mountains by J. R. Morse, Orrin Merrill, and C. R. Hakes. Eager miners quickly arrived at the newly-discovered site of wealth and threw up their tents or constructed crude paloverde-pole shacks. More permanent wooden structures were erected by enterprising merchants.

The boom was on. As fortune hunters poured into Goldfield, the rudimentary camp acquired the embellishments of a more civilized community. A school supplied the educational needs of the children and Reverend Clarke looked after the spiritual growth of the populace. One Sunday the clergyman preached to fifty attentive listeners in Goldfield's leading saloon.

Goldfield soon followed the same path taken by many other boom camps. For some reason, the mine closed. People began to move elsewhere and Goldfield died.

In 1909 or 1910 the site of Goldfield came to life again, but under the name Youngsberg. George U. Young, secretary of Arizona and acting governor at the time, secured and further developed the mine property. He installed a stamp mill and cyanide plant at the Goldfield Mine and supplied the new camp with bunkhouses and a boardinghouse. The ore was low-grade and the renewed attempt ended in failure.

Today the site is occupied by a curio shop and a few concrete foundations.

Goldflat

COUNTY: *Mohave*
LOCATION: *3 mi. southwest of Kingman*
MAP: *page 175*
P.O. est. Goldflat, Dec. 22, 1908; discont. July 15, 1910.

Goldflat, a small community, functioned as a result of the Gold Flat Mining and Milling Company. It seemed to have been short-lived, leaving few indications of its former existence. In 1909 Goldflat reported a population of sixty-five, and a blacksmith, barber, carpenter, hotel, general merchandise store, livery stable, and restaurant.

Goldroad

COUNTY: *Mohave*
LOCATION: *30 mi. southwest of Kingman*
MAP: *page 175*
P.O. est. as Acme, April 15, 1902; changed to Goldroad, March 24, 1906; discont. Oct. 15, 1942.

Jose Jerez, grubstaked by Henry Lovin, a Kingman merchant, located the Goldroad Mine about 1899. As the story goes, Jerez stumbled upon the gold outcrop while tracking his burros, which had strayed from camp.

Gold was first discovered in the area by John Moss in 1863. Although the Moss Mine stimulated prospecting, somehow the Goldroad outcrop was overlooked. Then, during the '80's, attention shifted to the silver ore in the Cerbat range, so it was not until Jerez's find that miners hurried back into the previously-prospected region.

After Jerez and Lovin sold the mine in 1901, considerable work on the property generated the active, prosperous community of Goldroad. Businesses and dwellings sprang up to form a community of four hundred citizens. Jose Jerez seemed to have disappeared from the scene, but Henry Lovin stayed around and reaped greater wealth in the new camp by erecting and owning the Gold Road Club and a general merchandise and freighting company.

Goldroad Mine produced mostly low-grade ore. After about thirty years, work stopped. Goldroad is now reduced to rocks, rubble, and roofless, doorless, rock and adobe buildings.

Goldroad—present-day ruins of a once thriving mining town.

Goldroad, *circa* 1918. Over $7,000,000 worth of gold was mined in this camp between 1903 and 1931.
—*Courtesy Thomas McMichael*

Advertisement, 1910.—*Courtesy Lillian Sweetland*

AT THE TOWN HALL
Goldroad
Thursday and Friday Nights
March 10th and 11th, 1910

MORE CLASS
SOWERS & LANG'S
Great Motion Picture Show
Greater, Better and Bigger Than Ever

Little Italy

A Romance in the Italian colony in New York. A true
picture of real Italian life.

Husband's Strategy
AND
Helpmate

of the finest class pictures ever shown in the Southwest.

Briton and Boer

A wonderful picture of the Boer War. Have you ever seen
a South African mine? If not, you will be able to see the
great DE BEER'S mine to-night in Motion Pictures.
Other pictures as good, if not better, will be shown.
Don't miss this opportunity to see some of the greatest
pictures ever produced in the Motion Picture World.

Prices, 20 and 35 cents

Advertisement. — *Courtesy Arizona Pioneers' Historical Society*

View of the main street of Goldroad, *circa* 1918.—*Courtesy Thomas McMichael*

Goldroad, *circa* 1918. After the sacks of ore were weighed they were loaded on burros for the trip to the stamp mill.—*Courtesy Thomas McMichael*

Greaterville

COUNTY: *Pima*

LOCATION: *about 45 mi. southeast of Tucson in the Santa Rita Mountains*

MAP: *page 195*

P.O. est. as Greaterville, Jan. 3, 1879; discont. June 30, 1946.

An 1874 discovery of placer gold by A. Smith produced a rush into the area and organization of the Greaterville mining district. Within a few years almost four hundred Mexicans and a hundred Americans had settled in the newly established village of Greaterville. The rich gravels were eagerly worked until the 1880's, when the gold supply was considered depleted. In the early years of Greaterville's boom, miners panned more than $10.00 a day in gold. Since water was scarce, a few Mexicans made a living packing canvas bags of water by burro from Gardner Canyon.

Greaterville may have lacked refinement, but it did not want for necessities. Several dance halls, saloons, and stores filled most of the miners' needs. Deputy Sheriff Bob Kerker and Justice of the Peace Patrick J. Coyne maintained law and order. The jail was a round hole dug in the ground, into which offenders were lowered by means of a rope. Patrick Coyne also taught a night school until Greaterville's first public school was started in 1882. At that time, only two other schools existed in Pima County.

About seven miles east of Greaterville was the Empire Ranch. Occasionally the Mexicans of Greaterville would organize a *baile* (dance) and the ranch cowboys would attend. Once when the Empire boys arrived they found a *baile* in full swing behind locked doors. The Mexican miners had decided they did not want to share their girls with any of the cowboys, and refused to let them inside. The ranch group was not going to be so easily denied an evening of dancing. Watching the smoke from a cozy blaze billow from the fireplace chimney of the dance hall, one of the cowboys concocted a clever plan. Climbing on top of the roof, he dropped a handful of revolver cartridges down the chimney. Minutes later, as the hot cartridges exploded, the scared Mexicans burst out through the doors and windows. The Empire boys quickly grabbed the fleeing *señoritas*, thus acquiring partners for the next dance. One Mexican *hombre*, who resented losing his girl to a cowboy, jealously proceeded to follow his rival around the dance floor with a knife ready for action. Immediately behind him was a cowboy with a drawn Colt, ready to protect his Empire buddy if necessary. Fortunately it was not necessary, and the dance ended without violence. After the *baile*, the owners of the ranch extended a cordial invitation to the Mexicans and their families to be their guests at the Empire Ranch at an early date.

Although the prosperous years of Greaterville's life were soon over, renewed mining activity every now and then kept the settlement from dying completely. Greaterville is now reduced to a handful of houses occupied by a few Mexican families.

Greaterville, date unknown. Water being transported from Gardner Canyon to the placer mines—Bags were made of heavy duck, with horn handles on the bottom.—*Courtesy Arizona Pioneers' Historical Society*

Greaterville, 1896. In the foreground, a party of Papago Indians who came once a year to sell pottery. They had been dancing for provisions. —*Courtesy Arizona Pioneers' Historical Society*

Greaterville, 1898—the Downer store and post office at the right.—*Courtesy Arizona Pioneers' Historical Society*

Greaterville, 1896. The barn in the center had been used as a post office at Total Wreck before it was moved to Greaterville.—*Courtesy Arizona Pioneers' Historical Society*

Greenwood City

COUNTY: *Mohave*
LOCATION: *about 20 mi. south of Wikieup*
MAP: *page 177*
P.O. none.

The famous McCracken (McCrackin) silver mine was discovered on August 8, 1874, by Jackson McCracken, a member of the Walker party. A ten-stamp mill to crush the McCracken ore was erected twelve miles from the mine on the Big Sandy River. The new mill proceeded to form the nucleus for Greenwood City. As the excitement grew, following the discovery of the McCracken, prospective settlers arriving at the new milling site quickly transformed it into a bustling town of enthusiastic activity.

For the next two years, Greenwood City continued to expand, eventually attaining a population of four hundred people. Among the attributes of the place were the well-patronized Davis House (where travelers were offered clean beds and luxurious meals), two of the nicest saloons in the country (owned by Fatty Smith and John Cody), two large blacksmith shops, grocery stores, a butcher shop, a barber shop and a physician. Less desirable in a community of that size was the fact that Uncle Sam never provided a post office. Therefore, citizens paid out over $1,000 a year to private mail carriers.

Sometime after 1878, when a new twenty-stamp mill was established at neighboring Virginia City to work the McCracken ore, Greenwood City's mill became obsolete. Afterward, little or nothing was reported of the once-active milling center.

Gunsight

COUNTY: *Pima*
LOCATION: *17 mi. southeast of Ajo*
MAP: *page 185*
P.O. est. as Gunsight, June 27, 1892; discont. Jan. 6, 1896.

The Gunsight Mine, named for its location near a mountain formation resembling a gun sight, was discovered in 1878. It proved to be a rich silver producer. Miners attracted to the new operation formed Gunsight camp. By 1892, the town was prospering under the Silver Gert Mining Company. Forty men were employed and eight buildings had been constructed by the company. A nearby ranch furnished Gunsight residents with vegetables and dairy products, and a tri-weekly stage ran between the camp and Gila Bend.

Advertisement. — *Courtesy Arizona Pioneers' Historical Society*

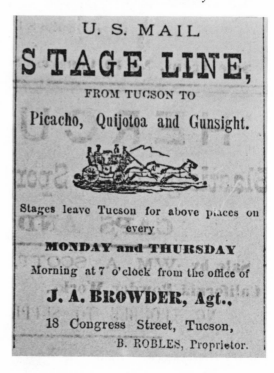

Gunsight — present-day ruins on the north slope of the Gunsight Mountains.

Hamburg

COUNTY: *Cochise*
LOCATION: *16 mi. south of Sierra Vista*
MAP: *page 195*
P.O. est. as Hamburg, Oct. 5, 1906; discont. (?).

A mining community that flourished for a number of years in Ramsey Canyon was named for its founder, Henry Hamburg, a German from St. Louis. Hamburg supported about 150 people, many of whom were miners employed by the mining companies developing the area. Saloons, boardinghouses, general stores and dwellings of one sort or another comprised the town. A stage line to Hereford was maintained, the Huachuca Trading Company operated a business in groceries and clothes, the Hartford-Arizona Copper Mining Company owned a hotel and general merchandise store, and W. J. Berner apparently made a living as a florist.

Henry Hamburg was president of Princeton Copper and business manager for Hartford-Arizona Copper, two of the mining companies reported working at Hamburg.

Exactly when the place became a ghost town is uncertain, but nothing is left of it today.

Hardyville

COUNTY: *Mohave*
LOCATION: *7 mi. south of Davis Dam*
MAP: *page 175*
P.O. est. as Hardyville, Jan. 17, 1865; discont. Feb. 19, 1883.

Hardyville was once a ferry crossing, the head of practical navigation on the Colorado River, an important distributing point for freight and supplies for interior mining districts, a trading center and rendezvous for miners, and the first seat of Mohave County.

William Harrison Hardy, a native of Watertown, New York, came to California with a wagon train in 1849. He was elected captain of the company and thereafter familiarly known as Captain Hardy. By 1864, Hardy, who had accumulated a fortune through mercantile pursuits, purchased the Colorado River Ferry. He erected a well-stocked store, hotel, saloon, warehouse, and a few adobe shanties on the Arizona side of the river, and

Hardyville was born. It was never a large place. There were only about twenty permanent residents, but often there were many transients passing through the town.

Hardy was a well educated man of wide vision, well-bred, generous with his wealth, popular, and respected among those who knew him. Although he had purchased the ferry as a business investment and ran it for profit, if a person had no money, Hardy would kindly give a free ferry pass. In addition to his ferry and the town, Hardy also maintained and operated a toll road between Hardyville and Prescott. Maintenance was no problem. Hardy merely walked along the road and kicked aside any obstructive rocks.

One of the many enterprises for which Captain Hardy was noted was the invention of riveted mail sacks. In the early days of pony mail, the mail sacks were carried behind the horse's saddle. The thread used to sew the sacks frayed easily and the sacks would rip open. As onetime postmaster of Hardyville, Hardy would send the ripped mail bags to his harness shop and have them riveted. During a trip to Washington, D.C., Hardy had a talk with the Postmaster General and recommended that the mail sacks be made with rivets. His suggestion was adopted, and that procedure used ever since.

Twice Hardyville suffered from fire. In November, 1872, the steamer *Cocopah* arrived in Ehrenberg with news of the burning of Hardyville. Again in March, 1873, a totally destructive fire swept through the small river landing. Although partially rebuilt, the town was eventually doomed when a railroad crossing was constructed at Needles, California, in 1883. The buildings of the community have long since vanished.

The Colorado Steam Nav. Co.

Will Dispatch

THE LARGE PALATIAL and MAGNIFICENT

STEAMER MOHAVE.

which

will leave Yuma for El Dorado Cañon and intermediate points on SUNDAY MAY 1st., at 9 o'clock A. M., Parties desiring freight or passage by this STEAMER will please call at the Company's Office in the Railroad Depot foot of Main Street.

J. P. KNAPP Agent C. S. N. Co.

| S. P. R. R. | A LORETTE. | YUMA, |

Steamer dedication announcement.—*Courtesy Arizona Pioneers' Historical Society*

William Harrison Hardy (1823–1906). —*Courtesy Arizona Pioneers' Historical Society*

Harqua Hala

COUNTY: *Yuma*
LOCATION: 12 *mi. south of Salome*
MAP: *page 177*
P.O. est. as Harqua Hala, March 5, 1891; discont. Aug. 31, 1918. Re-est. as Harqua, June 6, 1927; discont. Dec. 31, 1932.

More than a century before the discovery of the Bonanza and Gold Eagle veins, gold was known to exist in the Harquahala Mountains. A party of Spanish prospectors in 1762 were first to find the wealth, but hostile Indians quickly put an end to their mining endeavors. A second attempt in 1814 likewise proved disastrous to those concerned. Not until November of 1888 were the two locations staked that nurtured Harqua Hala. Accredited with the discoveries were Harry Walton, Robert Stein, and Mike Sullivan. The Bonanza and the Golden Eagle veins immediately lured miners, merchants, and the inevitable boom-town followers. A stage line operated from the newly formed Harqua Hala settlement to Sentinel. There were stores, saloons (the first of which was started by a man with a small tent and a five-gallon jug of whisky), and eventually a newspaper, the *Harqua Hala Miner*.

The mining property came into possession of Hubbard and Bowers, who erected a twenty-stamp amalgamation mill. Another improvement, made from an idea conceived by Hubbard's engineers, was the ingenious casting of gold into four-hundred-pound bars. Gold bullion cast in ordinary molds of fifteen to twenty ounces each had to be put under heavy convoy when shipped to Phoenix, but protection could be minimized if bars were made too heavy to steal easily. Once, while being transported, a four-hundred-pound ingot broke through the flimsy wagon bottom, unbeknownst to the driver and his companion. A few miles farther on, the driver looked back and realized his valuable cargo was gone. When the gold bar was found at the bottom of a gully, it proved to be a task requiring both ingenuity and strength for the two men to retrieve their treasure and get it back to the road and safely into the wagon.

Supposedly, a certain amount of quiet high-grading was done at the Harqua Hala Mine. On signal, a group of the camp children would raise their voices in song, drowning out the sound of their fathers scraping the arrastra beds for residual gold.

The Harqua Hala Gold Mining Company acquired the mine property in 1893. Four years later the ore body was exhausted. There followed a succession of owners and lessees who worked the mine intermittently over the next forty years. During that time, Harqua Hala camp gradually withered into a cluster of deserted buildings and ruins.

Harqua Hala, looking east at present-day ruins.

Harrisburg. Memorial to California pioneers massacred in 1849 by Indians and buried by passing emigrants, later to be known as the Harrisburg Cemetery.

Harrisburg

COUNTY: *Yuma*
LOCATION: *5 mi. southeast of Salome*
MAP: *page 177*
P.O. est. as Harrisburg, Feb. 9, 1887; discont. Sept. 29, 1906.

Harrisburg was founded in 1886 by Captain Charles Harris, former Canadian and Civil War veteran, and Arizona's Territorial Governor Tritle. By November of that year, two companies, the Ore Milling & Mining and the Harris Milling & Mining were established at Harrisburg and employed a large number of men. Other miners were equally happy developing their own properties in the vicinity. Although a mere embryo in 1886, Harrisburg already gave promise of becoming one of the liveliest camps in the Territory. The sought-after status, obviously based on speculation, was never realized.

More enduring, and perhaps more historically interesting than the camp itself, is the Harrisburg cemetery. Adorning the cemetery is a white quartz rock monument topped by a silhouette of a covered wagon, placed there in memory of a band of pioneers who were brutally massacred by Indians. In the years before the establishment of the mining community the site of Harrisburg was marked only by a waterhole. During the California gold rush in 1849, a covered wagon party stopped one night to camp near the waterhole. Months later, their burned wagon and bleached skeletons were found by another group of emigrants, who carried the bones to a small knoll and buried them. During Harrisburg's life other graves were added to the cemetery, but as time passed the graves were neglected and forgotten. It was not until 1936, when the weed-filled graveyard was accidentally rediscovered, that an effort was made to officially honor the victims of the early tragedy. The Arizona State Highway Department cleared the cemetery and erected the memorial.

Harshaw

COUNTY: *Santa Cruz*
LOCATION: *about 10 mi. southeast of Patagonia*
MAP: *page 195*
P.O. est. as Harshaw, April 29, 1880; discont. March 4, 1903.

David Tecumseh Harshaw, a cattleman, settled at a place known as Durasno in 1873. Having some knowledge of and interest in mining, Harshaw turned his attentions to prospecting. His efforts proved profitable. Gradually a mining community formed, and Durasno was renamed Harshaw in honor of David Harshaw, who had become a prominent citizen.

The Hermosa Mine was the lifeblood of Harshaw. First located in 1877, the mine was sold a year or two later to the Hermosa Mining Company of New York, which erected a twenty-stamp mill. From October, 1880, to November, 1881, the Hermosa Company operated the mine, using 150 men.

During those two prosperous years, Harshaw was in its prime. Lining the main and only street for three-fourths of a mile were eight or ten stores, lodginghouses and hotels, corrals, blacksmith shops, and (according to a one-time resident) thirty saloons. A town newspaper, the *Arizona Bullion*, established by Charles D. Reppy and Co., furnished Harshaw residents with items of local news and other matters.

A series of cloudbursts which caused material damage, a major fire, and the closing down of the mine by the Hermosa Mining Company in 1881 contributed to a temporary slump in Harshaw's economy. When the mine was bought by James Finley of Tucson for six hundred dollars in 1887, Harshaw acquired its second wind. Although it never attained its former peak of prosperity, the town persisted, with fewer citizens. A school, two stores, a meat market, three saloons, three boarding-houses, a livery stable, and a blacksmith shop still operated. There were about twenty-five private houses and a hundred residents.

Finley worked the Hermosa Mine for a number of years and then lessees took over until 1903. At that time the market value of silver declined. Finley died, and work stopped. A few families lived on in Harshaw, and a few still live there today.

Harshaw, 1962.—*Courtesy Arizona Pioneers' Historical Society*

Construction of the Hermosa Mill, Harshaw, 1879.—*Courtesy Arizona Pioneers' Historical Society*

A class of children at the Harshaw School, 1892.—*Courtesy Arizona Pioneers' Historical Society*

Helvetia, 1901. Looking east over the camp toward the Santa Rita Mountains.
—*Courtesy Arizona Pioneers' Historical Society*

Helvetia

COUNTY: *Pima*
LOCATION: *about 30 mi. southeast of Tucson*
MAP: *page 195*
P.O. est. as Helvetia, Dec. 12, 1899; discont. Dec. 31, 1921.

The Old Frijole Mine, located by Bill Hart and John Weigle in 1880, is the oldest mine in the Helvetia district. Work on the Frijole and other nearby mines started during the 1880's. When the Helvetia Copper Company of New Jersey acquired many of the claims in 1891, Helvetia camp began forming.

The motley cluster of tents and adobe and grass shanties comprising Helvetia was situated below the picturesque backdrop of the Santa Rita Mountains. The population, mostly Mexican, appears to have fluctuated with the camp's ups and downs, but the peak was probably three hundred. Helvetia embraced the usual assortment of saloons and stores, a school, and stage lines to Tucson and Vail.

In 1903 the Helvetia Copper Company of Arizona took over the mining operations. A 150-ton smelter was built, but did not prove successful, and was shut down after a couple of years. The low price of copper in 1911 resulted in the closing of the mines.

A few deserted adobe and wood buildings and a cemetery are all that remain at Helvetia.

Typical makeshift grass dwellings, Helvetia, 1902.—*Courtesy Arizona Pioneers' Historical Society*

Helvetia—deserted building.

Hilltop

COUNTY: *Cochise*
LOCATION: *14 mi. south of San Simon*
MAP: *page 199*
P.O. est. as Hilltop, Jan. 26, 1920; discont. June 30, 1945.

The original location of the Hilltop Mine in the Chiricahua Mountains was made by Jack Dunn in the early 1880's. Frank and John Hands acquired the property in the 1890's and sold it to the Hilltop Metal Mining Company in 1913. The ensuing months produced active mining development in the area and the establishment of Hilltop on the northwest slope of Shaw Peak.

The pride of Hilltop in 1913 appears to have been a new seven-passenger six cylinder Cole automobile, purchased by the company. A commodious garage was built exclusively for Hilltop's automobile and supplied with all necessary tools for keeping the machine in top running order.

In 1917 a tunnel was driven through to the northeast side of the mountain, where a larger townsite for Hilltop was started. A number of well-constructed wooden buildings, including bunkhouses, a manager's house, dance hall, pool hall, and restaurant, soon embellished new Hilltop.

Work on the Hilltop Mine was curtailed after 1926. Although various companies controlled the mine until 1949, there was little production. Meanwhile, Hilltop had served its purpose. The town reported a hundred people in 1930, but the number gradually dwindled, allowing Hilltop to fall into its present state.

Hilltop, 1920. (1) Power house and machine shop; (2) dance hall and card room, located on the east slope of the Chiricahua Mountains.—*Courtesy Ralph Morrow*

Hilltop, 1920. A level spot had to be blasted from the mountain slope to provide room for the home of the mine manager. — *Courtesy Ralph Morrow*

Ruins of bunkhouses and the machine shop as they exist today in Hilltop.

Howells

COUNTY: *Yavapai*
LOCATION: *about 12 mi. south of Prescott*
MAP: *page 189*
P.O. est. as Howells, Feb. 15, 1883; discont. Nov. 16, 1893.

Howells, functioning as a small mining camp and smelter site during the 1880's, consisted of a general store, saloon, and post office. Mail arrived at Howells tri-weekly, and a stage and express route was maintained between the camp and Prescott. Situated beside Lynx Creek in the Bradshaw Mountains, Howells reported fifty residents in 1888.

Jerome

COUNTY: *Yavapai*
LOCATION: *6 mi. west of Clarksdale*
MAP: *page 187*
P.O. est. as Jerome, Sept. 10, 1883.

Clinging to the precarious slope of Mingus Mountain slumbers Arizona's famous ghost city, Jerome. Copper, the source of Jerome's wealth and prosperity, once boosted the fabulous metropolis to the fifth-largest city in Arizona. Now merely a shadow of its grandiose past, Jerome imports tourists instead of exporting copper.

The first scrapings of minerals on Mingus Mountain can be traced back to the year 935 and the Tuzigoot Indians. They were after the brilliant blue azurite and pigments for body, garment, and pottery decorations. Copper itself was of no interest or worth. The neglected metallic ore would have to wait for centuries before white men arrived and placed a high value on it. Nevertheless, the Indians played a small role, for they left behind a good-sized hole in the mountain which was found by Antonio de Espejo in 1583 and by Marcos Farfan de los Godos in 1598. They both looked at the Indians' shaft and then left. All they wanted was gold.

This does not appear to be a very auspicious beginning for Jerome, but everything changed with the arrival of Al Sieber. General Crook's able scout, Sieber, knew the value of copper. In 1876 he staked the first claim on Mingus Mountain, but failed to develop it. Another claim filed that same year by M. A. Ruffner and Angus McKinnon really started the boom. Probably because they could not finance the mine, it was leased to Governor Tritle of Arizona. Seeing that development was impossible without adequate backing, Tritle interested James A. MacDonald and Eugene Jerome of New York in forming a company. Jerome's only stipulation was that the mining town be named for him. In 1882 the United Verde Company was formed.

The next two years were profitable ones. The mine development progressed, and Jerome began to evolve and expand. Then the value of copper took a tumble in 1884, and the mine closed. Apparently it did not affect the growth rate of Jerome, since the first school was started that year. It was

a short-lived slump, however, for Montana's Senator William A. Clark was attracted by the United Verde, soon bought the mine, and began the intensive mining operations that quickly reaped fame and fortune for Jerome.

As copper demands increased, bringing about a steadier price level, Jerome flourished. Three fires —in 1897, 1898, and 1899—momentarily retarded Jerome's high spirits, but the damage was always repaired for the better. Jerome was incorporated in 1899. That year the city's business inventory reported some of the following: four grocery stores, five confectionery and fruit stands, six dry goods stores, six lodging houses, eleven restaurants, seventeen saloons, a hardware store, a tailoring shop, a bank, two bakeries, two jewelry stores, two drugstores, a telephone company, and all types of professional men, with skills from photography to dentistry.

Considering the rough type of characters attracted to mining communities and the amount of liquor they usually consumed, Jerome maintained fairly good law and order. A scuffle occurred once between Jack Habercorn, known as "Happy Jack," and Bob Williams. It resulted in Jack stabbing his adversary with one of those now old-fashioned pointed miner's candlesticks. The act, prompted by an insult, fortunately produced only a minor injury, but a trial was held in one of the saloons. Presiding over the court was Justice of the Peace Major Oatie. When the jury found "Happy Jack" guilty, it was up to Major Oatie to pass sentence. Since it was the judge's first trial held in Jerome, he doubtless felt a certain amount of leniency was in order. "Happy Jack" was fined the drinks for the house.

An incident causing a certain amount of excitement was the arrival of two strangers in town one Sunday in November of 1900. They were toting in a wagon what they said was a petrified man. Naturally the story had to be good, or the strangers would not benefit from their profit-making scheme. The stone image was taken to St. Elmo Saloon, where it was displayed for gullible curiosity seekers. Day and night men crowded into the saloon to gaze at the remains of the great and strong man obviously shot down in the prime of his life. The owner of the petrified man not only could point out where the bullet hole was, but also could elaborate in detail about how the man had been buried in a lime deposit. So convincing was the image that many people were fooled. The owner, extremely pleased with himself, got hilariously drunk and wound up in jail. After being bailed out by two sympathetic souls who advanced $10.00 to pay the fine, the owner and his companion hauled away the petrified man to places unknown, and the excitement subsided.

Jerome's peak population of fifteen thousand was reached just prior to the depression years. As the price of copper went hurtling downward, the United Verde Mine closed in 1932, and work ceased. The outlook for Jerome began to appear hopeful again in 1935, when the Phelps-Dodge Corporation purchased the mine property and resumed operations. Yet, the past glory and fame would never come again. Phelps-Dodge shut down the mine in 1950. Jerome seemed doomed. It might have been the end had not a group of enterprising citizens organized the Jerome Historical Society and proclaimed Jerome to be America's newest and largest ghost city.

Today Jerome attracts thousands of visitors annually. Perhaps Jerome's uniqueness is due to the fact that ever since a huge dynamite blast in 1925, the town has been gradually slipping downhill. Some buildings, having moved many feet from their original locations, contribute greatly to Jerome's attraction for tourists.

Early Jerome (1880).—*Courtesy Sharlot Hall Museum*

Jerome, 1913. On the east slope of Mingus Mountain, Jerome became one of the largest mining towns in the West. — *Courtesy Arizona Pioneers' Historical Society*

Inside of George Laman's saloon, Jerome, 1897.—*Courtesy Arizona Pioneers' Historical Society*

Jerome, 1899. At one time, hose cart racing was quite popular. In this photograph the Jerome Fire Department is taking part in such activities. — *Courtesy Arizona Pioneers' Historical Society*

Dr. Hawkins' dental office, the saloon, and the Grand View Hotel on Jerome's Main Street (date unknown). — *Courtesy Sharlot Hall Museum*

Advertisement.—*Courtesy Arizona Pioneers' Historical Society*

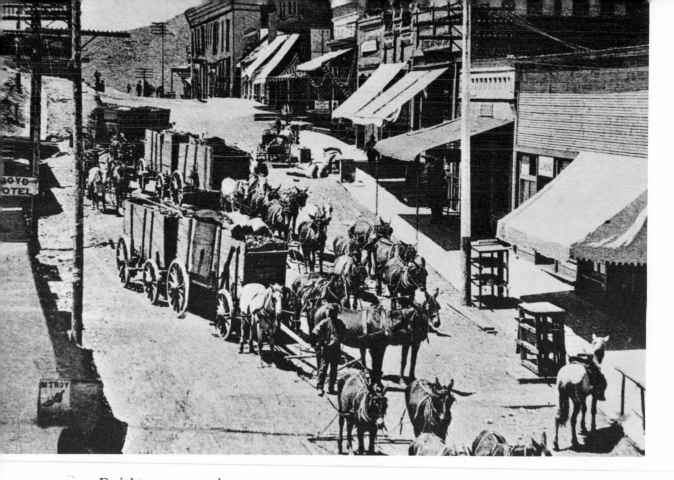

Freight wagons and teams on
Main Street of Jerome, 1911.
—*Courtesy Arizona Pioneers'
Historical Society*

Jerome, *circa* 1920.—*Courtesy
Arizona Pioneers' Historical Society*

Jerome—a present view of the
cemetery, looking across the
Verde Valley.

Jerome, Arizona's largest ghost city.

Johnson

COUNTY: *Cochise*
LOCATION: *19 mi. northeast of Benson*
MAP: *page 195*
P.O. est. as Johnson, April 5, 1900; discont. Nov. 29, 1929.

Founded as the headquarters for the Peabody Company in 1883, Johnson was the successor to nearby Russellville. Mr. Johnson, the town's namesake, was general manager of the company at that time. By July, 150 men were employed working the copper from the Peabody Mine, and Johnson had blossomed into a clustering of saloons, stores, and other establishments. The best business in the camp was the company's boardinghouse, competently run by Mrs. Hanson. Unfortunately, she was obliged to dispose of her job in order to go to California for surgical treatment. The poor woman had the misfortune to shoot herself in the foot.

Most mining camps seem to lure a certain number of hangers-on and saloon bums. Johnson apparently had some of these characters. On a December evening in 1883, Colonel Mike Smith and a man named Mason were returning to Johnson from Dragoon Station, where they had just cashed their pay checks. Some unknown parties concealed along the roadside began to take pot shots at the two. Both riders escaped unharmed, but their horses were wounded. The attempted robbery was believed to be the doing of some Johnson idlers of questionable reputation.

Having acquired the essentials of a mining camp, Johnson slipped into the twentieth century with apparent ease. A mining slump followed the turn of the century, but work resumed again about 1909, and Johnson accelerated its pace of development. By 1925 it had become a bustling community of a thousand people.

In addition to the Peabody, there were many other companies working and developing the area's copper wealth. Three other mines in the vicinity were the Black Prince Copper, Cochise Copper, and Keystone.

The mid-twenties were good years. Suddenly, the depression dropped the price of copper, and Johnson's life ended.

Little more than a few concrete foundations are left. There are also some headframes and other signs indicating previous mining.

Johnson—Headframe and mill buildings of the Keystone Mine.

Katherine, *circa* 1919. Cyanide processing tanks under construction at the Katherine Mine. Buildings of the camp are seen in the left background.— *Courtesy Mohave Pioneers' Historical Society*

Katherine

COUNTY: *Mohave*
LOCATION: *about 5 mi. northeast of Davis Dam*
MAP: *page 175*
*P.O. est. as Katherine, Dec. 21, 1921; discont.
June 5, 1929.*

The Katherine Mine was discovered in September, 1900, by S. C. Baggs and developed by the New Comstock Mining Company. The ore was treated at the Sheep Trail Mill at Pyramid, on the Colorado River. In 1904 the Arizona-Pyramid Gold Mining Company acquired the mine-mill property and began a more extensive development program. Little profit was made during these early years, because of the expense of wagon transportation and the relatively inefficient amalgamation process used. Operations were suspended in 1906. When the Katherine Gold Mining Company took over in 1919, active exploration resumed at the mine. A new shaft was sunk, and a 150-ton cyanide mill built at the mine.

The gold mine began to attract a crowd to Katherine camp. Single miners and married men as well were induced to settle in Katherine. As part of the promotion to lure a growing population, a free town lot was offered to the parents of the first female baby born at the camp. There was one provision to the generous offer—the child must be given the name Katherine.

In the 1930's, Katherine boasted of becoming one of the most comfortable camps in the country. It had a big boardinghouse, large enough to feed the entire working crew in thirty minutes.

The mine is still visible, but there does not appear to be anything left of Katherine.

Kofa

COUNTY: *Yuma*
LOCATION: *about 45 mi. southwest of Quartzsite*
MAP: *page 179*
P.O. est. as Kofa, June 5, 1900; discont. Aug. 27, 1928.

In 1896, Charles Eichelberger was prospecting in the southwestern edge of the S. H. Mountains (now Kofa Mountains). Finding he was nearly out of water, Charlie headed up a canyon in search of a tank—a rock basin containing rain water. After a strenuous climb, he located a tank, filled his canteen, and sat down to rest. While idly scanning the canyon, Charlie saw a shiny object about twenty feet away, so he walked over to investigate. It proved to be the gold outcropping that later developed into the famous King of Arizona Mine. Eichelberger soon joined forces with H. B. Gleason and Epes Randolph and organized the King of Arizona Mining Company.

By June of 1897 a five-stamp amalgamation mill had been completed near Mohawk, on the Gila River about thirty-five miles south of the mine, and miners were busily working at the King. The mine, still too young to have nurtured a town that first summer, did not offer the miners any accommodations. They slept out in the open, or in a cave if anybody was fortunate enough to find one. The men working the graveyard shift faced the problem of trying to sleep during the day with no protection from the hot summer sun. Water was also a problem. For two days their drinking water was sloshed around in old wine and whisky barrels as a mule team hauled it from wells at Mohawk. It tasted terrible and made many miners ill, but it was all they had.

The mine was too rich to allow a few inconveniences to hinder development, and before long, everything began to change. Quite a settlement sprang up at the mine. Named Kofa (abbreviation for King of Arizona), it embraced a boardinghouse, bunkhouse, company store, saloons, and a school. Many miners and families were now making Kofa their home.

A scarcity of water still prevailed. After several fruitless attempts at deep drilling, a water supply was struck about five miles south of the King. The company then constructed a 100-ton mill and cyanide plant at the mine. Later the mill was enlarged to a capacity of 250 tons, and 125 men were employed on the King of Arizona property.

Cornishmen, Mexicans and Chinese seem to have made up the working force of Kofa. The "Cousin Jacks" were the miners, the Mexicans chopped and sold wood for running the mill, and the Chinese were the cooks for the company.

Kofa was not a bad place, but felonies occasionally did occur. Joaquin Nogales tried to burn down some buildings at Kofa and got six years for attempted arson. "Pinky Dean," a drunken Negress, slashed up a miner with a knife in her apartment back of a saloon.

The mine and mill were actively run until July, 1910. By that time the mine was exhausted, and the tailings were not worth reworking, so all was shut down.

Kofa, 1902. — *Courtesy Yuma County Historical Society*

BULLION SHIPMENT
KING OF ARIZONA MINE
G H ROCKWOOD

Kofa, date unknown.—*Courtesy Arizona Pioneers' Historical Society*

King of Arizona Mill and the men who operated it, Kofa, 1910.—*Courtesy Yuma County Historical Society*

Kofa cemetery and Kofa Butte.

La Paz

COUNTY: *Yuma*

LOCATION: *7 mi. north of present-day Ehrenberg*

MAP: *page 177*

P.O. est. as La Paz, Jan. 17, 1865; discont. March 25, 1875.

Captain Pauline Weaver, noted Arizona frontiersman, discovered placer gold near the Colorado River in 1862. Going to Fort Yuma for supplies, Weaver told of his find. The news spread like wildfire, producing an immediate stampede to the new district. Miners rushing to the gold site were not disappointed. The placers were rich and extensive. The miners stayed, built La Paz, and worked the rich gravels for about seven years.

The first surge of people flooding into the area had little to eat besides mesquite beans and fish, but it did not matter. Gold was the answer to all problems. In the evenings miners and gamblers would spread their blankets on the dusty street and play cards for the heavy nuggets.

During La Paz's infancy, a thief who had been stealing from stores was apprehended. There being as yet no law officer, the citizens held a meeting to decide the culprit's fate. He was sentenced to twenty-five lashes. After these were promptly given, they handed the thief $5.00 and told him to get out of town. Thereafter the community was not troubled with stealing.

La Paz grew by leaps and bounds. A year later the town, thronging with Mexicans, Indians and white men, numbered about fifteen hundred citizens. It became an important landing and freighting point on the Colorado River, and was the county seat of Yuma County until 1871.

Stores were established by Gray and Company, Joseph Goldwater, and Isaac Goldberg. Assorted occupations included blacksmith, baker, gardener, barber, liquor dealer, physician, harnessmaker, lawyer, brewer, and shipmaster.

Gradually the Colorado River changed its course, leaving La Paz abandoned as a steamboat landing. Placer gold began to give out, and people scurried away to the more promising settlement of Ehrenberg, six miles down-river.

The adobe buildings deteriorating through the years were wiped out by a flood about 1910.

Steamer *Gila*. Put into service in 1877, the *Gila* was typical of the stern wheelers on the Colorado River.—*Courtesy Arizona Pioneers' Historical Society*

La Paz, *circa* 1891, at that time a ghost town.—*Courtesy Arizona Pioneers' Historical Society*

Pauline Weaver (1800–67). —
Courtesy Sharlot Hall Museum

Eventually, supposedly the same community on the Arizona-Sonora border acquired the name of Lochiel, by which it is still known. Now just a sleepy little settlement nestled among cottonwood trees and containing a handful of people and a U.S. Customs Station, Lochiel was once a lusty mining camp and one of Pancho Villa's rustling spots. In addition to the smelter and considerable mining in the area, the community flourished on stock raising. Pancho Villa and his men made easy profits by raiding the herds and rustling the stock into Mexico.

Lochiel also marks the place where the first European west of the Rockies, Fray Marcos de Niza, a vice commissary of the Franciscan Order and delegate of the viceroy of Mexico, entered what is now Arizona on April 12, 1539. A monument is erected in his honor.

Lochiel

COUNTY: *Santa Cruz*
LOCATION: *24 mi. east of Nogales*
MAP: *page 195*
P.O. est. as Luttrell, Aug. 23, 1880; discont. Feb. 19, 1883. P.O. est. as La Noria, July 24, 1882; discont. June 11, 1883. P.O. est. as Lochiel, Oct. 6, 1884, changed to La Noria, Dec. 17, 1909; discont. Sept. 30, 1911.

References seem to indicate that Lochiel, La Noria, and Luttrell might well have been the same place. If not, their sites were so close together they can hardly be separated. In January of 1881, Luttrell claimed to be the site of the Holland smelting works and a settlement of four hundred people within a radius of six miles, with five stores, three saloons, a brewery, a butcher shop, a bakery, and livery stables. Almost two years later, La Noria reports being the location of two smelters, the Holland and the Yankee, and a town of stores, saloons, and a boardinghouse run by Dr. Luttrell —no doubt the same man for whom the camp of Luttrell was named.

Francisco "Pancho" Villa (1877–1923), Mexican Revolutionist.—*Courtesy Arizona Pioneers' Historical Society*

McCabe

COUNTY: *Yavapai*
LOCATION: *about 6 mi. west of Humboldt*
MAP: *page 189*
P.O. est. as McCabe, Dec. 31, 1897; discont. Oct. 31, 1917.

Assorted piles of wooden boards, brick and corrugated iron sheeting, concrete ruins of a mill, tin cans, broken glass, and a dreary cemetery indicate the location of McCabe.

In the 1890's the McCabe gold mine, producing profitable results, encouraged the growth of the white tents and brown cabins dotting the hillsides and gulch. Even before a post office was established, McCabe camp was acquiring metropolitan airs, with a telephone line running to Prescott, a daily stage from Prescott, and a three-time weekly stage from Phoenix.

McCabe was a typical mining camp of three hundred to six hundred persons. Dr. Robert N. Looney, McCabe's physician for a number of years, arrived in 1896 and erected a small six-bed hospital. A one-room schoolhouse functioned for the children.

Several fires occurred during McCabe's history. One broke out just before midnight on July 5, 1900. Starting in Jerry's Last Chance Saloon, it spread rapidly, consuming fourteen buildings.

In May of 1901, McCabe experienced a smallpox epidemic and a quarantine barrier was established. Just prior to that time, Mrs. James Broyles of Ash Fork had gone to visit her brother in McCabe. While there, he was stricken with the disease, and Mrs. Broyles was required to remain as a guest in his home until the quarantine was lifted. James Broyles, left alone in Ash Fork without his wife, was none too happy about the situation, so he decided to do something about it. Late one night Broyles sneaked into his brother-in-law's house and got his wife. The next day, when Mr. and Mrs. Broyles were seen on the streets of Prescott, the fact that she had not been officially liberated from the quarantined home came to light. The case was brought before Judge Moore, who listened attentively to James Broyles' plea of guilty and then fined him a hundred dollars. After both husband and wife were sprayed with an antiseptic, they departed for Ash Fork.

In 1913 the McCabe Mine closed. With the main sustaining force of the camp gone, people gradually left and McCabe died.

McCabe, *circa* 1905. Development of one of McCabe's gold and silver mines—note the horse-powered winch.—*Courtesy Sharlot Hall Museum*

McCabe-Gladstone Mine and McCabe, looking north, 1905.—*Courtesy Sharlot Hall Museum*

Lane Maine Boarding House, McCabe, *circa* 1905.—*Courtesy Sharlot Hall Museum*

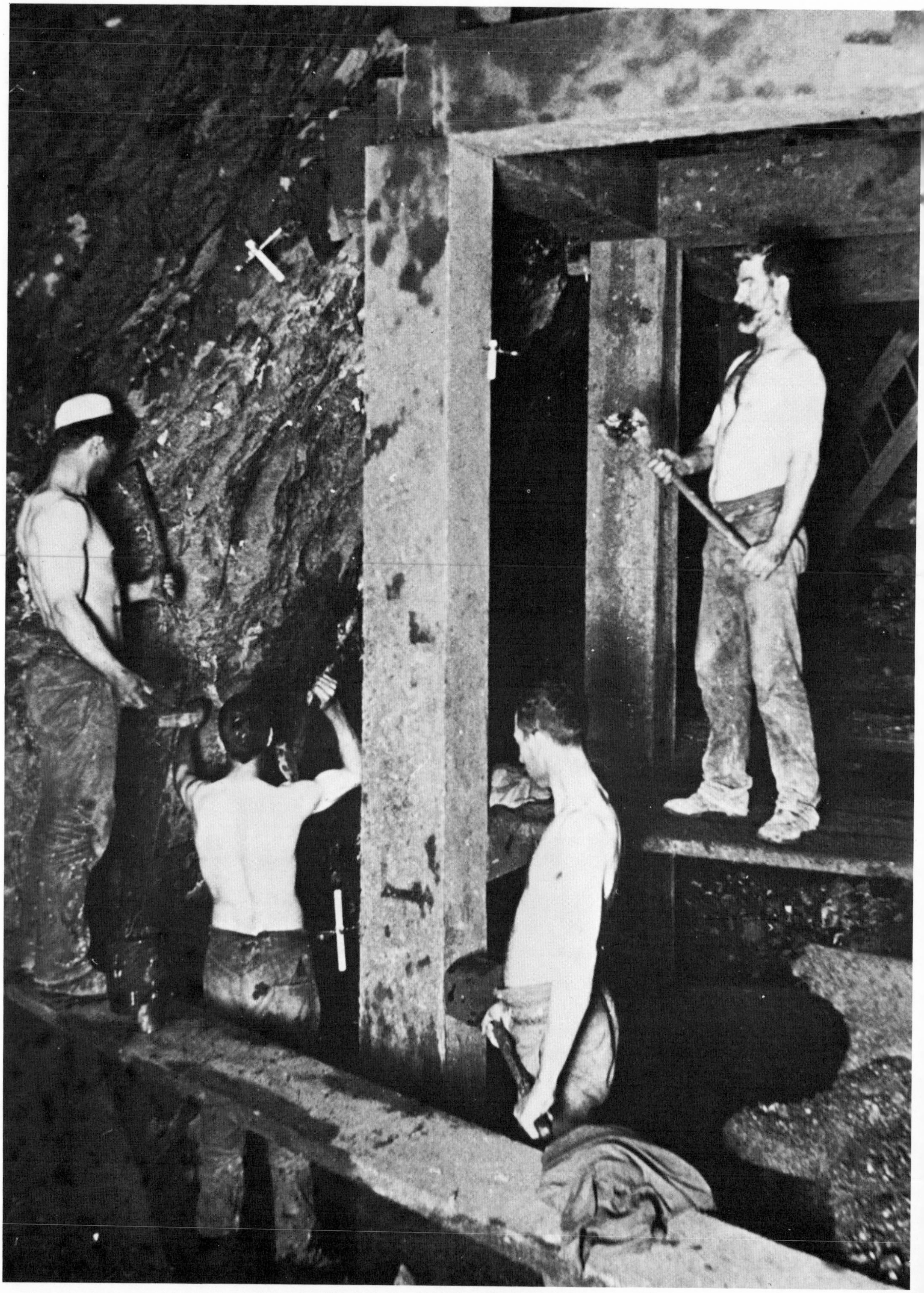

Square set mining, *circa* 1885. Scenes such as this were common in early underground mining.—*Courtesy Arizona Pioneers' Historical Society*

McMillenville

COUNTY: *Gila*
LOCATION: *about 28 mi. north of Globe*
MAP: *page 191*
P.O. est. as McMillenville, Nov. 12, 1877; changed to McMillen, Oct. 11, 1878; discont. Oct. 12, 1882.

Many mines have been discovered purely by accident. The Stonewall Jackson was one of these.

On March 6, 1876, Theodore (Dory) H. Harris and Charles McMillen were heading northeast from Globe to the White Mountains on a prospecting trip. As legend has it, McMillen had spent the previous night in riotous drinking. Finding himself a bit too groggy to continue any farther, he slid off his horse and plunged into a spot of shade to sleep. Harris, irritated by his indulgent friend, sat down on a ledge to wait. Idly driving his pick into the rock, he broke off a chunk matted with native silver. They staked a claim and named their find the Stonewall Jackson.

As the news leaked out, hundreds of people flocked to the Stonewall Jackson, creating McMillenville. In a short time, the camp embraced a thousand people and was the general supply center for neighboring mining claims. Temporary shanties and tents, hastily erected, were replaced by more permanent adobes. Shops, saloons, boardinghouses, dance halls, and gambling casinos sprang into existence. It was a noisy, busy, ambitious place.

The first killing in McMillenville resulted from a disagreement over a mining claim. Jack Brown, locator of the claim, naturally assumed ownership. However, the fact was disputed by another man. One night, after considerable argument over the issue, the two faced each other on the main street, drew their guns, and fired. Their aim was true. Seconds later both lay stone dead, feet to feet.

McMillenville was at a prosperous peak in 1880. The original five-stamp mill at the mine was soon replaced by twenty-stamps, and up-to-date hoisting works were erected at the shaft. Freight wagons loaded with the Stonewall Jackson's silver ingots traveled the hundred miles to the nearest railroad shipping point at Casa Grande. There was plenty of work and plenty of profit.

Hostile Apaches attacked McMillenville in 1882. Fortunately, the camp had been forewarned and was able to make advance preparations. Women and children were assembled and ushered into a Stonewall Jackson tunnel for protection, with an able body of men standing guard. All other males gathered in Pat Shanley's two-story adobe building, well armed and ready to ward off the raiders. At daybreak of July 7, the Indians arrived. With yells and war whoops, the attack began. Luck was on the white men's side. The sharpshooting McMillenville residents kept the Indians at bay until soldiers arrived from Fort Apache. At sight of the military men, the savages realized they were outnumbered and abandoned their target. Casualties on the McMillenville side amounted to one man shot in the arm, a number of burned buildings, and fifteen slaughtered cattle.

McMillenville's life was almost over. By 1885 the silver pay streak was exhausted, and the camp followed the inevitable path to oblivion.

Little is left today but ruins of three buildings, rubble near the mine, and some concrete foundations.

Metcalf

COUNTY: *Greenlee*
LOCATION: *about 8 mi. north of Clifton*
MAP: *page 197*
P.O. *est. as Metcalf, Aug. 25, 1899; discont. May 15, 1936.*

Metcalf was once a prosperous copper town tucked between the granite cliffs of Chase Creek Canyon. Now at least half of the site has been buried by the giant, expanding tailings pile of the huge Morenci Copper Mine. Many rock retaining walls, rock and concrete foundations, one large concrete building, adits, and tunnels clearly show Metcalf's former locale.

Robert Metcalf, reconnoitering as a scout for Captain Chase in 1870, struck a rich copper deposit not far from the company's camp near the present site of Clifton. Conditions at that time prevented Metcalf from pursuing his find, but he promised himself he would return as soon as possible to stake a claim. Two years later a party led by Bob Metcalf and his brother, Jim, located the famous Longfellow Mine.

The Metcalfs sold out to the Leszinsky brothers from Las Cruces, New Mexico, who began developing the property. They erected an adobe furnace in Chase Creek Canyon, but it proved to be unprofitable and was replaced by a water jacket smelter at the mouth of the canyon. Transportation of the ore from the mine to the new smelter created a problem. It was solved with the construction of a twenty-gauge railroad winding up the floor of the canyon to connect with a gravity incline at the mine. The Leszinskys purchased a diminutive wood-burning locomotive from Pittsburgh, Pennsylvania. After being shipped around the Horn to San Francisco, thence to Yuma, and overland to Clifton, the tiny engine—christened "The Coronada" but affectionately known as "Little Emma" —was placed on the tracks.

The Arizona Copper Company took over operations in 1882. Before long, the town of Metcalf had taken root and expanded into an extensive community. Four or five thousand people composed the population. Included in the town were a bank, school, hospital, dairy, pool hall, and movie theater.

The depression years brought Metcalf's story to an end. Mines closed, people left, and the townsite eventually became the dumping ground for the Morenci pit.

PACKING LUMBER METCALF ARIZ.

Metcalf, 1915.—*Courtesy Arizona Pioneers' Historical Society*

Shannon Copper Mine and Metcalf, 1903.—
Courtesy Arizona Pioneers' Historical Society

Singlejack drilling in a stope of the Wilson
Copper Mine, Metcalf, 1903.—*Courtesy
Arizona Pioneers' Historical Society*

Metcalf, 1903—tramming ore from the portal of one of Metcalf's many underground
mines.—*Courtesy Arizona Pioneers' Historical Society*

Middlemarch

COUNTY: *Cochise*
LOCATION: *about 9 mi. west of Pearce*
MAP: *page 195*
P.O. est. as Middlemarch, May 10, 1898; discont. Dec. 31, 1919.

Middlemarch was sustained by copper. The Cobreloma Consolidated and the Middlemarch Copper companies both operated here. There were about a hundred people, a general store, and a post office.

The name Middlemarch is accredited to the fact that the location was the midway point on the military route between Fort Bowie and Fort Huachuca. Rock walls, a long neglected steam boiler, and assorted debris and dumps still survive.

Millville

COUNTY: *Cochise*
LOCATION: *8 mi. southwest of Tombstone*
MAP: *page 195*
P.O. est. as Millville, May 26, 1879; discont. May 3, 1880.

Millville, situated on the east bank of the San Pedro River directly opposite the town of Charleston, was the location selected by Richard Gird for a mill to process the ore from the Tombstone silver mines. Millville and Charleston are often considered one and the same, but Millville served as a millsite, whereas Charleston served as a townsite.

There are a few ruins at Millville today. The most prominent are some high adobe walls which were once a large company office building. In 1882, M. R. Peel, a mining engineer for the Tombstone Mining and Milling Company, was seated in the office talking with three friends when the door was flung open and two gunmen fired at Peel. He slumped over, dead. The killers made no attempt to harm Peel's companions, nor did they try to rob the office. Having accomplished their deed, they fled into the night. There seemed to be no motive for this cold-blooded murder. Officials recorded it as an attempted robbery.

As Charleston became the larger of the two towns, Millville's post office was discontinued. People left Millville when water flooded the Tombstone mines and the mills stopped working.

Richard Gird, Al Schieffelin, and Ed Schieffelin, *circa* 1875. The three partners discovered and developed the Lucky Cuss, Toughnut, and Contention mines around Tombstone during the early 1870's.—*Courtesy Arizona Pioneers' Historical Society*

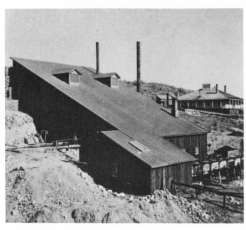

Millville, *circa* 1873. Gird's Mill, foreground; company office where murder occurred, background.—*Courtesy Arizona Pioneers' Historical Society*

The Tombstone-Millville Pony Express, *circa* 1873.—*Courtesy Arizona Pioneers' Historical Society*

Birds-eye view of the operations at Millville, *circa* 1880. Charleston can be seen in the right background.—*Courtesy Arizona Pioneers' Historical Society*

Mineral Hill

COUNTY: *Pima*
LOCATION: *16 mi. south of Tucson*
MAP: *page 195*
P.O. dates unknown.

The camp at Mineral Hill never had a chance to develop fully because mining was too sporadic. From 1882 to 1884, Emperor Copper Company exploited the copper deposits on Mineral Hill, but a slump in the copper market caused the operations to be discontinued. About 1897, Azurite Copper and Gold Company was organized, and a year later the company erected a thirty-ton smelting jacket at the mine. A camp was formed near the smelter. Known as Azurite, it was composed mostly of Mexican miners and laborers. Many tents, a number of frame buildings, and a store were probably the extent of the small community. Azurite increased to a population of 125 by March of 1899, and reported the need for appointment of a peace officer, since liquor conveniently smuggled into camp and consumed by the Mexicans was causing the working schedules to be disrupted.

By 1900 the mine had closed and Azurite camp ceased to exist. The mine property remained idle for six years, until it was purchased by Mineral Hill Consolidated Company. At that time Mexican miners were being paid $2.00 to $2.50 a day for a ten-hour shift. Operations were short-lived, however, for work stopped in 1907.

Some mining resumed during World War I. In the early 1920's, Mineral Hill claimed a store and a post office.

Mineral Park

COUNTY: *Mohave*
LOCATION: *about 19 mi. northwest of Kingman in the Cerbat Mountains*
MAP: *page 175*
P.O. est. as Mineral Park, Dec. 23, 1872; discont. June 15, 1912.

A five-stamp mill was erected and the townsite of Mineral Park was laid out in 1871. Some two hundred men, actively engaged in building adobe houses, grading lots, and working in the mines, gave the new camp an air of promise and prosperity. No time was lost in establishing the necessary institutions of gambling and whisky. Within a few months, seven saloons had sprung to life, and a public school, several stores, and a post office followed.

Mineral Park, located in the center of a rich and extensive silver mining region, grew into the largest settlement in Mohave County. With its rapid growth, the town acquired prominence and importance. Not only did it serve as an indispensable supply center for mining camps and cattle ranges, but in 1877 it became the seat of Mohave County.

By the early 1880's, Mineral Park bustled with activity. The ore was rich, and when the railroad was completed, transportation was cheap. The mines were yielding immense profits, soaring Mineral Park's economy to a high peak. Lawyers, doctors, blacksmiths, carpenters, and a justice of the peace added their trades and professions to the town. More stores, a hotel, restaurant, and weekly newspaper, the *Mohave County Miner*, were established as the population increased to seven hundred.

The Walapai Indians living in and around Mineral Park were not particularly troublesome, nevertheless, they were held in low esteem by many people. Once in 1882, Walapai Charley, a leader of the Walapai tribe, drew his gun on a fellow Indian named Jeff. Jeff went to Undersheriff Collins and lodged a complaint against Charley. In an effort to ease the situation, Collins brought Charley into his office, confiscated the offender's side arm, and warned him never to show his face in town again unless he wished to be clapped into jail. The next day Sheriff Robert Steen received the following letter:

Walapai Charley's Camp
My Friend Bob Steen
Won't you be so kind as to send me my pistol. I will not carry it into town anymore and will behave myself and be a good Indian. Tell me when I can come into town and oblige.

Your Friend Walapai Charley.

Although there are a few ruins still left and a picturesque cemetery, a large portion of old Mineral Park is presently occupied by the buildings and operations of Duval Mining Company.

Mineral Park Cemetery as preserved by the Duval Mining Company.

Mineral Park, circa 1880.— Courtesy Mohave Pioneers Historical Society

Mohave City

COUNTY: *Mohave*
LOCATION: *about 10 mi. south of Bullhead City*
MAP: *page 175*
P.O. est. as Mohave City, Oct. 8, 1866; discont. Oct. 31, 1938.

Located on the Colorado River about a mile north of Fort Mohave, the town was laid out and built primarily by the California Volunteers stationed at the fort in 1863. Serving as a river landing and trading center, Mohave City acquired greater importance in 1866 when it was made the seat of Mohave County. People came, built homes, and established businesses without any interference until the fall of 1869. At that time the boundary of the military reservation was extended to engulf Mohave City. Consequently, orders were issued for all Mohave City residents to evacuate the reservation within thirty days. The people reluctantly closed homes and stores and hauled their possessions off to new locations. The military took over at once, occupying some of the buildings and tearing down others.

From that time on, the place was referred to as Mohave City or Fort Mohave, since both were one and the same.

In the 1880's the community listed a variety of trades among its fifty residents. Some of these were a gunsmith, blacksmith, druggist, shoemaker, and tailor. Business must have been profitable, because Paul Breon, owner of the general store and postmaster at Mohave City, could afford to take his San Francisco bride to Vienna for their honeymoon.

Sometime later an Indian school was established, but today nothing remains of the city, fort, or school.

Mohave City, 1904. Colorado River landing accommodating travelers to Mohave City.— *Courtesy Arizona Pioneers' Historical Society*

Mowry, *circa* 1864. Headquarters at the Mowry Mine, from J. Ross Browne, *A Tour Through Arizona, 1864*, New York, Harper Bro., 1869.

Mowry

COUNTY: *Santa Cruz*
LOCATION: *about 14 mi. south of Patagonia*
MAP: *page 195*
P.O. est. as Patagonia, May 7, 1866; discont. Nov. 22, 1880. P.O. re-est. as Mowry, June 23, 1905; discont. July 31, 1913.

The Patagonia Mine, located by Mexicans in 1858, changed owners several times before it was purchased in 1860 by Lieutenant Sylvester Mowry, an army officer stationed at Fort Crittenden. Mowry renamed the mine for himself, erected smelting equipment, furnaces, and buildings, employed Mexican laborers, and successfully worked the lead-silver mine for a number of years.

Operations were ruthlessly interrupted in 1862, when Lieutenant Mowry was arrested by General James H. Carleton and charged with selling lead to the Confederate Army to be used for ammunition. Mowry was confined to the Yuma Territorial Prison from July 2 to November 8 of that year. On his release, Mowry went to England, where he hoped to get money to recommence his operations, but while he was there, he died.

During the Civil War years the Apaches went on a raiding rampage. They succeeded in driving out most white men in the Patagonia region, destroying the Mowry smelting works, and reducing the settlement to ruins.

New owners eventually brought the mine and the community of Mowry back to life. It was prospering when the town became the focal point for a big Fourth of July celebration in 1891. Excited visitors from the surrounding area and Nogales began convening at Mowry on the evening of the third. A fund of $340 had been collected for fireworks, to be freighted in for the occasion. The day's events included speeches, singing, races, and dancing.

In 1904 the Mowry Mines Company took over the property. Considerable expansion and improvements were made. The town reported some five hundred residents, stores, saloons, and a schoolhouse. A post office under the name Mowry was established in 1905.

Today, Mowry consists of a deserted cluster of rapidly deteriorating adobe and wood buildings. A small cemetery is located on a knoll not far from the town.

Sylvester Mowry (1832–71).—*Courtesy California State Library*

Mowry, *circa* 1864—the Mowry camp, from J. Ross Browne, *A Tour Through Arizona, 1864.* New York, Harper Bro., 1869.

Mowry Mine and part of the camp, 1909, looking northwest. The mill is at the right and the smelter is at the left.—*Courtesy U.S. Geological Survey*

Mowry—one of the old camp buildings as seen today.

Present-day ruins of Mowry.

Nugget

COUNTY: *Gila*
LOCATION: *about 10 mi. north of Globe*
MAP: *page 191*
*P.O. est. as Nugget, Jan. 7, 1881; discont.
    March 10, 1884.*

In the late 1860's, a German named Schulz located the Nugget Mine in Richmond Basin. Not realizing the value of silver, he traded the claim to the Chilson brothers of Globe for a mule. The Chilsons were soon shipping high-grade silver ore to San Francisco.

Nugget was the small mining camp supported by the mine. There was a post office, a saloon and a couple of general merchandise stores.

Oatman

COUNTY: *Mohave*
LOCATION: *32 mi. southwest of Kingman*
MAP: *page 175*
P.O. est. as Vivian, March 1, 1904; changed to Oatman, June 24, 1909.

Oatman is not completely deserted. Although the boom is over and the buildings and people have dwindled in number, the town lures rock hounds, photographers, and curious tourists to its picturesque setting below jagged rock promontories.

About 1902, Ben Paddock discovered the Vivian Mine. The property came into possession of the Vivian Mining Company in 1903, and the community of Vivian began to evolve. There were several stores, two banks, a Chamber of Commerce, and about 150 people.

In the early years, when Oatman was still known as Vivian, a story is told of the courageous tenacity of a miner who lost his eyesight. Henry Ewing continued to work his Nixon Mine, located near Vivian, despite his handicap and the warnings of concerned friends. He set up guide wires to assure himself a degree of safety, and then proceeded to sink a shaft. Completely unaided, Ewing drilled, blasted, mucked, hauled ore buckets to the surface, and cared for himself at his camp. He experienced two narrow escapes with death, once when he unexpectedly encountered a rattlesnake, and another time when he fell thirty feet from a ladder.

With the discovery of the Tom Reed gold mine in 1908, the town became known as Oatman. The post office name was changed from Vivian to Oatman in 1909, and a sense of prosperity and renewed excitement began to permeate the area.

Oatman allegedly was named in honor of Olive Oatman, a white girl taken captive by Indians in 1851. After enduring unimaginable hardships for five years, she was released through the efforts of her brother, Lorenzo, the only surviving member of her family, who were brutally massacred by Indians.

The opening of the United Eastern in 1913 really started Oatman's boom. Buildings mushroomed everywhere as the population climbed to ten thousand residents. Oatman's heyday years ran well into the 1930's.

Oatman, *circa* 1920. View of the Tom Reed Gold Mine and Oatman. This mine is known to have produced over $13,000,000 worth of gold between 1907 and 1933. — *Courtesy Lillian Sweetland*

Gold Shipment, *circa* 1918. Photographed in front of Lovin and Wither's Store, Front Street, Kingman, Arizona.—*Courtesy Mohave Pioneers Historical Society*

Oatman, *circa* 1930, looking south along Main Street toward the Boundary Cone.—*Courtesy Lillian Sweetland*

Main street of Oatman, *circa* 1935.—*Courtesy Lillian Sweetland*

Oatman—a building that was refurbished for the motion picture "How The West Was Won." Note that this building and the one in the center of the above photograph are the same.

Ruins of Octave, looking west toward Congress Junction.

Octave

COUNTY: *Yavapai*
LOCATION: *8 mi. east of Congress Junction*
MAP: *pages 183-189*
P.O. est. as Octave, April 19, 1900; discont. Dec. 31, 1942.

Octave, a mining camp located in the vicinity of Rich Hill, came into existence in the late 1890's. Although claims were staked at Rich Hill in 1864, the Octave Mine was not developed until some three decades later when it was purchased by a group of eight men who organized the Octave Gold Mining Company.

Little is left today of the community that once supported a school, post office, grocery store, general merchandise store, and stage line. When the mine was closed after World War II, the buildings were razed in order to reduce taxes.

Old Glory

COUNTY: *Santa Cruz*
LOCATION: *about 25 mi. west of Nogales*
MAP: *page 195*
P.O. est. as Oldglory, Jan. 15, 1895; changed to Old Glory Nov. 23, 1909; discont. Aug. 14, 1915.

Active mining in southern Santa Cruz County close to the Mexican border prompted the establishment of the Oldglory post office. Evidently the community was large enough to warrant a justice of the peace and a general merchandise store. Arizona Consolidated Mining Company and Gold Mining Association Company operated here. In 1905 the population was reported to be fifty inhabitants.

Oldtrails

COUNTY: *Mohave*
LOCATION: *1 mi. south of Oatman*
MAP: *page 175*
P.O. est. as Oldtrails, Feb. 29, 1916; discont. July 21, 1925.

To commemorate the famous trails which once linked early settlements, the National Old Trails Association and the Daughters of the American Revolution marked old trails. A now-vanished community located on one of these trails was appropriately named Oldtrails.

Oldtrails burst to life within four months during the spring of 1915. Situated near not only the famous Tom Reed and United Eastern mines, but also many other great mining properties, the new town grew rapidly, soon reaching a population of five hundred.

The town boasted of more than just the necessities of a mining camp. There were electric lights, graded streets, a district hospital, steam laundry, wholesale ice cream and bakery shop, bottling works, sheet metal works, and telephone and telegraph connections.

Oldtrails had every apparent reason to be an ideal settlement, but gradually the future began to look less promising, as mining prospects dimmed. By 1925, with only a handful of people remaining, the post office closed.

Today two buildings remain at Oldtrails. One is an old motel and service station recently converted into a restaurant. The other, a stone house, was once an assay office, but is now a private home.

Olive

COUNTY: *Pima*
LOCATION: *17 mi. south of Tucson*
MAP: *page 195*
P.O. *est. as Olive, March 4, 1887; discont.
    May 23, 1892.*

Named in honor of Olive Stephenson Brown,
Olive was an active silver camp during the 1880's
and 1890's. Serving such mines as the Olive, San
Xavier, Wedge, Michigan Maid, and Richmond,
the camp was unique in that there was no mill,
smelter or machinery. Ore was merely extracted
and sent elsewhere to be processed, and the miners
received their returns by check.

Olive Brown, whose husband James Kilroy
Brown was one of the owners of the Olive Mine,
gave more to the camp than just her name. While
living there, Mrs. Brown formed the habit of treat-
ing the employees of the Olive Mine to a free
chicken dinner every Sunday. Soon Sunday became a day of feasting and fun, and was eagerly
anticipated by the men. After the Olive Mine was
sold in the late 1880's, the Brown family moved
to Tucson.

The downfall of Olive camp was caused by the
switch from silver to copper mining.

Olive City

COUNTY: *Yuma*
LOCATION: *about 14 mi. south of Ehrenberg*
MAP: *page 179*
P.O. *none.*

Situated near a ferry landing on the Colorado
River, Olive City (or Olivia) was sometimes
known as Bradshaw's Ferry. William D. Bradshaw established a ferry in 1863, and was authorized to charge the following prices for transportation across the Colorado: wagon and two horses,
$4.00; carriage and one horse, $3.00; saddle
horse, $1.00; footman, $.50; live cattle and horses,
$.50 a head; and sheep, $.25 a head.

Olive City, composed of about a dozen assorted
buildings, lists a population of nineteen (all male)
in the 1864 census. Their occupations included
miners, one carpenter, one surveyor, one farmer,
one laborer, and a superintendent of mines.

Probably named for Olive Oatman, a white
girl held captive by Indians for five years, Olive
City was at one time considered the principal
town in the Weaver district. Since more than a
century has lapsed since the existence of the settlement, there is nothing left.

Olive Oatman—Olive City was named in honor of
Olive Oatman, whose family was massacred by the
Tonto Apaches in 1851. Olive was captured and
later sold to the Mohave Indians, who forced her
to take one of the braves as a husband. Five years
after her capture, when she was about twenty years
old, she was rescued through the efforts of her
brother. When forced to leave her Indian family
she became insane and reportedly died in an asylum
a few years later. Note the Indian tattoo marks on
her chin.—*Courtesy Arizona Pioneers' Historical
Society*

Abandoned dwellings at present-day Oro Belle.

Oro Belle

COUNTY: *Yavapai*
LOCATION: *about 45 mi. south of Prescott*
MAP: *page 189*
P.O. est. as Harrington, May 17, 1904; discont.
   Aug. 31, 1918.

Tucked in a valley of the mighty Bradshaw Mountains on the south slope of Wasson Peak nestle the deserted buildings of Oro Belle.

At one time, Oro Belle supplied the working force of a hundred men to mine the rich gold property of the Oro Belle and Gray Eagle veins. It was in the late 1890's, when George P. Harrington obtained the gold-bearing claims and organized the Oro Belle Mining and Milling Company, that

Oro Belle's history began. The most active years were from 1900 to 1910. Known as Harrington in those days, the camp had a population of about two hundred and an assortment of saloons, markets, and stores. A deputy sheriff and justice of the peace enforced laws and meted out justice.

George P. Harrington, the mine manager, was a plain, unassuming fellow, tremendously liked by all. His kindly nature prompted him to grubstake dozens of miners and to provide employment for those who sought jobs. In 1905 some of the major stockholders claimed that Harrington was too lavish in expenditures and replaced him with a more conservative manager, a mining engineer named Schlesinger. Harrington, however, remained at the mine as a sort of nominal advisor with no authority.

Once in command, Schlesinger embarked upon a pinchpenny reform program. Every conceivable method was employed to save money. The miners did not object to the new procedure until the quality and quantity of the boardinghouse food dropped far below palatable standards. As dissatisfaction grew, Schlesinger made a feeble agreement to improve the bill of fare, but promptly reneged on his word. Finally, one afternoon the boiling point was reached. Men erupted from the mine, mill, and boardinghouse, formed an angry mob, and ominously approached Schlesinger. Brooks Freeland, delegated as spokesman, stepped from the crowd, walked up face to face with Schlesinger and stated that unless the food was improved immediately they all would leave camp. Schlesinger, confronted by so many grim, dissatisfied faces, began to weaken. In a cowardly voice he promised to grant all requests and pleaded for enough time to bring in fresh food before they carried out their threat.

He may have brought the food, whether or not he did is not known, but the ending was happy. Schlesinger, having lost face with his employees, resigned his position as manager. Harrington was quickly reinstated, and once again Oro Belle became a cheerful and contented camp.

Oro Belle, *circa* 1898. View of the camp, looking west.— *Courtesy Sharlot Hall Museum*

Day shift at the Oro Belle Mine, 1898. — *Courtesy Sharlot Hall Museum*

Oro Blanco

COUNTY: *Santa Cruz*
LOCATION: *about 30 mi. west of Nogales*
MAP: *page 195*
P.O. est. as Oro Blanco, Oct. 2, 1879; discont. April 30, 1903. Re-est. June 25, 1908; discont. April 30, 1915.

There were two mining camps known as Oro Blanco. The first, located near the Oro Blanco Mine, thrived during the last two decades of the nineteenth century. When a mining revival occurred a few years after the Oro Blanco post office had discontinued, a new Oro Blanco post office and community was established at a location about ten miles north of "old" Oro Blanco camp.

In April, 1873, a group of men reopened the Oro Blanco Mine, near the Mexican border. The rich vein had been worked previously by Mexicans and Spaniards and, for some reason, had been abandoned.

Prospects looked good in the 1870's. As work recommenced on the derelict mine, a small camp sprang to life. By the end of the first year, forty miners and a cluster of ten houses made up Oro Blanco camp.

The mine was soon being worked day and night, and seven arrastras were in constant motion. With attention now focused on the Oro Blanco district, other mining possibilities began to be explored. The result was the development of the Warsaw group, Yellow Jacket Mine and Ostrich Mine.

The houses were made of stone, adobe, and other convenient materials. Many were probably makeshift shacks. The schoolhouse, only a crude hovel, had a brush roof and three walls, with the fourth side entirely open. Chairs and desks were missing, but the ground and some store boxes sufficed. On particularly cold days a bucket filled with embers was passed from one shivering child to another in an effort to provide some warmth.

By the mid-1880's, Oro Blanco had grown into a more mature village. Reportedly, three mining and milling companies, the Oro Blanco, Esperango, and Orion Silver, supplied employment. Two steam mills were operating. A dentist, blacksmith, physician, constable, justice of the peace, deputy sheriff, saloonkeepers, and merchants constituted some of the services and necessities of the town. The population had increased to 225.

One of the town's claims to fame was that in 1899 the richest man in Arizona was reportedly residing at Oro Blanco. James A. Robinson's vast fortune, acquired through land, mines, and cattle was estimated to be somewhere between $1,200,-000 and $1,800,000. When he was sixty-seven, Robinson had made an average annual income of $45,000 while he, his Mexican wife, and their family, lived on $500 a year.

Cemetery at "new" Oro Blanco, which can be seen in the right background.

Oro Blanco, date unknown. Gold Boulder Mine and a horse-operated winch a few miles north of the Mexican border near "old" Oro Blanco.— *Courtesy Arizona Pioneers' Historical Society*

Owens

COUNTY: *Mohave*
LOCATION: *about 4 mi. south of Wikieup*
MAP: *page 177*
P.O. est. as Owens, April 4, 1899; discont. Aug. 31, 1914.

Situated at the base of McCracken Hill, the camp was named for "Chloride Jack" Owen, who with Jackson McCracken discovered the famous Mc-Cracken silver mine in 1874. Owens camp was born less than two years later. There were several substantial frame buildings, a hotel, a store, and a saloon.

After its beginning, there is a gap in Owens' history. Little or nothing seems to have been reported of the camp until a post office was established in 1899.

In addition to mining, there were also farming and stockraising in the area. At one time the population was about 150 residents.

Paradise

COUNTY: *Cochise*
LOCATION: *5 mi. west of Portal.*
MAP: *page 199*
P.O. est. as Paradise, Oct. 23, 1901; discont. Sept. 30, 1943.

Paradise got under way with the formation of the Chiricahua Developing Company about 1901. By 1904 the settlement contained an alleged thirteen saloons, at least three general stores, a hotel and a jail.

The original jail was an open-air arrangement where prisoners were shackled to a long chain stretched between two trees. A more permanent structure seemed in order and was built. One of the occupants who served a short sentence was

Pablo Zuniga. A native of Mexico, Pablo supported his wife and half a dozen or more children by selling cords of wood which he packed into town on burros. Although his profits were meager, he managed to have enough money for "vino." Pablo's daily nips at the bottle resulted in his beating his wife and family, to let them know he loved them. They understood his way of showing affection, but to an outsider his actions were easily misconstrued.

One day a neighbor passing the Zuniga tent and hearing the commotion reported to Constable Mart Moore that Pablo was beating his wife. Pablo was arrested and thrown into jail. His wife, Maria, not understanding the reason for her husband's arrest, decided to take matters into her own hands.

Taking a monkey wrench, she twisted the bars out of the jail window. Pablo crawled out and proceeded to make a hasty but inebriated retreat up the mountainside. His escape might have gone unnoticed, but he stopped in view of the town to yell and curse all gringos—especially Mart Moore. Before Pablo knew what had happened, Constable Moore had saddled his horse, ridden up the mountainside, lassoed Pablo's feet and was dragging him back to jail, where he remained until he was sober. Prosecuting Pablo for wife-beating was out of the question. Maria refused to testify.

When the mines closed down in 1907, the boom was over, but Paradise continued to survive despite the decrease in populace. A few people still live in Paradise.

Upper left — Paradise, looking southwest across Paradise Valley.

Upper right—Paradise, *circa* 1907 — the main street. — *Courtesy Arizona Pioneers' Historical Society*

Lower — Stagecoach from Paradise to San Simon, *circa* 1900. Light coaches were often used on short runs between neighboring towns. — *Courtesy Arizona Pioneers' Historical Society*

Pearce

COUNTY: *Cochise*
LOCATION: *28 mi. south of Willcox*
MAP: *page 199*
P.O. est. as Pearce, March 6, 1896.

Cornishman Jimmie Pearce and his wife lived in Tombstone during its heyday. They were a hardworking and frugal couple. He worked as a miner, and she ran a boardinghouse. Between the two, they managed to save enough money to invest in a cattle ranch in Sulphur Springs Valley. Their two sons, who longed to be cowboys, had encouraged the idea.

While riding the range one day in 1894, Jimmie Pearce urged his horse up a hill, dismounted, and sat down to rest. Absentmindedly he picked up a piece of quartz and idly hammered away on the ledge where he sat. A small nodule broke loose, revealing rich gold. Jimmie named his find the Commonwealth and staked out five claims, one for each member of his family.

Although there are other versions of the discovery of the Commonwealth, the above story will suffice. The mine was unique in that it was one of the very few overlooked by prospectors of the 1870's, who had thoroughly combed the area.

For a while the rich silver-gold mine was worked as a family affair, while eager promoters restlessly looked on, hoping to get their hands on the bonanza. Finally, John Brockman, a banker from Silver City, New Mexico, came to terms with Jimmie. Pearce would allow Brockman ninety days to work and develop the property. If within the designated time-period Brockman could take out enough ore to pay Jimmie $250,000, the sale would be consummated. Sixty days later, the Commonwealth Mine no longer belonged to the Pearces. Before signing away her share of the property, Mrs. Pearce made the new owners agree to give her exclusive rights to operate the only boardinghouse at the mine. She did not propose to be out of a job.

The Commonwealth lured miners and merchants who formed the metropolis of Pearce. By 1919, with a population nearing fifteen hundred, an excellent school, restaurants, saloons, hotels, garages, and a motion-picture theater, Pearce was ranked third in importance among the business towns in Sulphur Springs Valley. Douglas and Willcox captured first and second places.

The mine closed in the thirties and people began to drift away. Pearce's great mining days were over. Today the once prosperous business district is reduced to a post office and an interesting combination country store and museum.

Pearce, *circa* 1910. The water wagon owned and operated by Jim Harper and Owen Williams brought water to Pearce to be sold to the inhabitants. —*Courtesy Arizona Pioneers' Historical Society*

Pearce, *circa* 1900—the Commonwealth Mill under construction. The big boilers were used to operate the milling machinery.—*Courtesy Arizona Pioneers' Historical Society*

In 1896, one of Pearce's first rooming houses, operated by Mrs. S. T. Carr, seated at the left. The dining room was constructed from the lumber of the old Tombstone Jail. —*Courtesy Arizona Pioneers' Historical Society*

Present-day ruins of Pearce.

Advertisement. — *Courtesy Arizona Pioneers' Historical Society*

Pinal

COUNTY: *Pinal*
LOCATION: *3 mi. southwest of Superior*
MAP: *page 191*
P.O. est. as Picket Post, April 10, 1878; changed to Pinal, June 27, 1879; discont. Nov. 28, 1891.

The mill town of Pinal was nurtured by and paralleled the life of the Silver King Mine.

Before Pinal existed, the site of the town-to-be was a cattle ranch belonging to L. DeArnett. In 1877 DeArnett sold the property to the Silver King Company for their mill. The location was ideal—only five miles from the mine and near ample water. At first the settlement which began to accumulate around the mill was known as Picket Post, named for nearby Picket Post Butte, also known as Tordilla or Tortilla Peak. By 1879 the name had been officially changed to Pinal. For the next decade Pinal grew by leaps and bounds.

From 1880 to 1881 there was an increase of 123 buildings. The young city soon claimed a school; two churches, a Methodist and a Catholic; two lodges, the Odd Fellows and the Masons; a bank; a brewery; hotels; a newspaper, the *Pinal Drill*; many different stores and shops; and professions running the gamut from doctors to preachers. Entertainment was supplied by saloons and gambling houses. There was hardly a need or want that Pinal was unable to supply or fulfill.

With silver running at a high premium, high-grading was a frequent occurrence. The teamsters had devised a system for transferring ore into other hands before reaching Pinal. As the mule teams plodded along on their way from the Silver King, the drivers would invariably speak roughly to the animals. Then, as if to punctuate their speech, they would throw a chunk of silver at the mules. This action took place while passing a friend, and naturally the fellow high-grader had to stop and inspect the rock that had either hit or missed the mule. By this simple method many a mule skinner acquired additional wealth.

Gradually, the diminishing ore and the decrease in the value of silver doomed Pinal. When the great mill stopped pounding, people packed up and left. In 1890 only ten souls remained where once there had been over two thousand. There is nothing left today.

Looking southeast across the mill and the town of Pinal, 1880.—*Courtesy Arizona Pioneers' Historical Society*

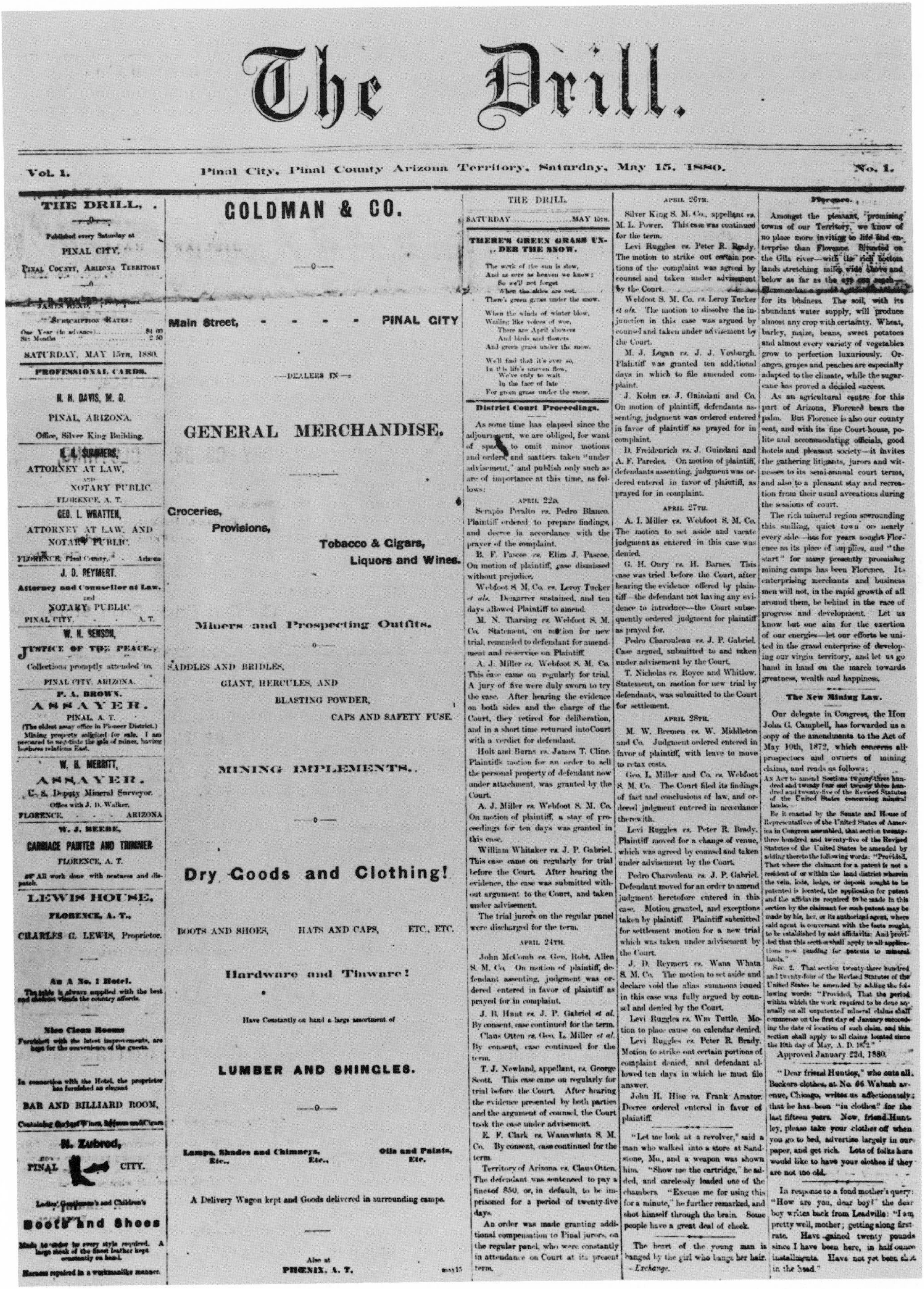

The Drill.

Vol. 1.   Pinal City, Pinal County Arizona Territory, Saturday, May 15, 1880.   No. 1.

THE DRILL,

Published every Saturday at
PINAL CITY,
Pinal County, Arizona Territory

JAMES REANY ......

SUBSCRIPTION RATES:
One Year (in advance) $4.00
Six Months 2.50

SATURDAY, MAY 15th, 1880.

PROFESSIONAL CARDS.

H. H. DAVIS, M. D.
PINAL, ARIZONA.
Office, Silver King Building.

U. C. SUMMERS,
ATTORNEY AT LAW,
AND
NOTARY PUBLIC.
FLORENCE, A. T.

GEO. L. WRATTEN,
ATTORNEY AT LAW, AND
NOTARY PUBLIC.
FLORENCE, Pinal County,   Arizona

J. D. REYMERT,
Attorney and Counsellor at Law,
and
NOTARY PUBLIC.
PINAL CITY,   A. T.

W. H. BENSON,
JUSTICE OF THE PEACE.
Collections promptly attended to
PINAL CITY, ARIZONA.

P. A. BROWN,
ASSAYER.
PINAL A. T.
(The oldest assay office in Pioneer District.)
Mining property solicited for sale. I am
prepared to negotiate the sale of mines, having
business relations East.

W. K. MERRITT,
ASSAYER.
U. S. Deputy Mineral Surveyor.
Offices with J. D. Walker.
FLORENCE   ARIZONA.

W. J. BEEBE,
CARRIAGE PAINTER AND TRIMMER.
FLORENCE, A. T.
☞ All work done with neatness and dispatch.

LEWIS HOUSE,
FLORENCE, A. T.,

CHARLES G. LEWIS, Proprietor.

An A No. 1 Hotel.
The table is always supplied with the best
and choicest viands the country affords.

Nice Clean Rooms
Furnished with the latest improvements, are
kept for the convenience of the guests.

In connection with the Hotel, the proprietor
has furnished an elegant

BAR AND BILLIARD ROOM,

Containing Choicest Wines, Liquors and Cigars.

H. Zubrod,
PINAL   CITY.

Ladies', Gentlemen's and Children's
Boots and Shoes
Made to order by every style required. A
large stock of the finest leather kept
constantly on hand.
Harness repaired in a workmanlike manner.

GOLDMAN & CO.

Main Street,   -   -   -   PINAL CITY

—DEALERS IN—

GENERAL MERCHANDISE.

Groceries,
Provisions,
Tobacco & Cigars,
Liquors and Wines.

Miners and Prospecting Outfits.

SADDLES AND BRIDLES,
GIANT, HERCULES, AND
BLASTING POWDER,
CAPS AND SAFETY FUSE.

MINING IMPLEMENTS.

Dry Goods and Clothing!

BOOTS AND SHOES,   HATS AND CAPS,   ETC., ETC.

Hardware and Tinware!

Have Constantly on hand a large assortment of

LUMBER AND SHINGLES.

Lamps, Shades and Chimneys,   Oils and Paints,
Etc.,   Etc.,   Etc.

A Delivery Wagon kept and Goods delivered in surrounding camps.

Also at
PHŒNIX, A. T.   may15

THE DRILL

SATURDAY .... MAY 15th.

THERE'S GREEN GRASS UNDER THE SNOW.

The work of the sun is slow,
And as sure as heaven we know;
So we'll not forget
When the skies are wet,
There's green grass under the snow.

When the winds of winter blow,
Wailing like voices of woe,
There are April showers
And birds and flowers
And green grass under the snow.

We'll find that it's ever so,
In this life's uneven flow,
We've only to wait
In the face of fate
For green grass under the snow.

District Court Proceedings.

As some time has elapsed since the adjournment, we are obliged, for want of space to omit minor motions and orders, and matters taken "under advisement," and publish only such as are of importance at this time, as follows:

APRIL 22D.

Serapio Peralto vs. Pedro Blanco. Plaintiff ordered to prepare findings, and decree in accordance with the prayer of the complaint.

B. F. Pascoe vs. Eliza J. Pascoe. On motion of plaintiff, case dismissed without prejudice.

Webfoot S. M. Co. vs. Leroy Tucker et als. Demurrer sustained, and ten days allowed Plaintiff to amend.

M. N. Tharsing vs. Webfoot S. M. Co. Statement, on motion for new trial, remanded to defendant for amendment and re-service on Plaintiff.

A. J. Miller vs. Webfoot S. M. Co. This case came on regularly for trial. A jury of five were duly sworn to try the case. After hearing the evidence on both sides and the charge of the Court, they retired for deliberation, and in a short time returned into Court with a verdict for plaintiff.

Holt and Burns vs. James T. Cline. Plaintiffs motion for an order to sell the personal property of defendant now under attachment, was granted by the Court.

A. J. Miller vs. Webfoot S. M. Co. On motion of plaintiff, a stay of proceedings for ten days was granted in this case.

William Whitaker vs. J. P. Gabriel. This case came on regularly for trial before the Court. After hearing the evidence, the case was submitted without argument to the Court, and taken under advisement.

The trial jurors on the regular panel were discharged for the term.

APRIL 24TH.

John McComb vs. Geo. Robt. Allen S. M. Co. On motion of plaintiff, defendant assenting, judgment was ordered entered in favor of plaintiff as prayed for in complaint.

J. B. Hunt vs. J. P. Gabriel et al. By consent, case continued for the term.

Claus Otten vs. Geo. L. Miller et al. By consent, case continued for the term.

T. J. Newland, appellant, vs. George Scott. This case came on regularly for trial before the Court. After hearing the evidence presented by both parties and the argument of counsel, the Court took the case under advisement.

E. F. Clark vs. Wanawhata S. M. Co. By consent, case continued for the term.

Territory of Arizona vs. Claus Otten. The defendant was sentenced to pay a fine of $50, or, in default, to be imprisoned for a period of twenty-five days.

An order was made granting additional compensation to Pinal jurors, on the regular panel, who were constantly in attendance on Court at its present term.

APRIL 26TH.

Silver King S. M. Co., appellant vs. M. L. Power. This case was continued for the term.

Levi Ruggles vs. Peter R. Ready. The motion to strike out certain portions of the complaint was argued by counsel and taken under advisement by the Court.

Webfoot S. M. Co. vs. Leroy Tucker et als. The motion to dissolve the injunction in this case was argued by counsel and taken under advisement by the Court.

M. J. Logan vs. J. J. Vosburgh. Plaintiff was granted ten additional days in which to file amended complaint.

J. Kohn vs. J. Guindani and Co. On motion of plaintiff, defendants assenting, judgment was ordered entered in favor of plaintiff as prayed for in complaint.

D. Freidenrich vs. J. Guindani and A. F. Paredes. On motion of plaintiff, defendants assenting, judgment was ordered entered in favor of plaintiff, as prayed for in complaint.

APRIL 27TH.

A. I. Miller vs. Webfoot S. M. Co. The motion to set aside and vacate judgment as entered in this case was denied.

G. H. Oury vs. H. Barnes. This case was tried before the Court, after hearing the evidence offered by plaintiff—the defendant not having any evidence to introduce—the Court subsequently ordered judgment for plaintiff as prayed for.

Pedro Charouleau vs. J. P. Gabriel. Case argued, submitted to and taken under advisement by the Court.

T. Nicholas vs. Royce and Whitlow. Statement, on motion for new trial by defendants, was submitted to the Court for settlement.

APRIL 28TH.

M. W. Bremen vs. W. Middleton and Co. Judgment ordered entered in favor of plaintiff, with leave to move to retax costs.

Geo. L. Miller and Co. vs. Webfoot S. M. Co. The Court filed its findings of fact and conclusions of law, and ordered judgment entered in accordance therewith.

Levi Ruggles vs. Peter R. Brady. Plaintiff moved for a change of venue, which was agreed by counsel and taken under advisement by the Court.

Pedro Charouleau vs. J. P. Gabriel. Defendant moved for an order to amend judgment heretofore entered in this case. Motion granted, and exceptions taken by plaintiff. Plaintiff submitted for settlement motion for a new trial which was taken under advisement by the Court.

J. D. Reymert vs. Wana Whata S. M. Co. The motion to set aside and declare void the alias summons issued in this case was fully argued by counsel and denied by the Court.

Levi Ruggles vs. Wm Tuttle. Motion to place cause on calendar denied.

Levi Ruggles vs. Peter R. Brady. Motion to strike out certain portions of complaint denied, and defendant allowed ten days in which he must file answer.

John H. Hise vs. Frank Amator. Decree ordered entered in favor of plaintiff.

"Let me look at a revolver," said a man who walked into a store at Sandstone, Mo., and a weapon was shown him. "Show me the cartridge," he added, and carelessly loaded one of the chambers. "Excuse me for using this for a minute," he further remarked, and shot himself through the brain. Some people have a great deal of cheek.

The heart of the young man is banged by the girl who bangs her hair.—Exchange.

Florence.

Amongst the pleasant, promising towns of our Territory, we know of no place more inviting to life and enterprise than Florence. Situated on the Gila river—with its rich bottom lands stretching miles wide above and below as far as the eye can reach—Florence has a great agricultural basin for its business. The soil, with its abundant water supply, will produce almost any crop with certainty. Wheat, barley, maize, beans, sweet potatoes and almost every variety of vegetables grow to perfection luxuriously. Oranges, grapes and peaches are especially adapted to the climate, while the sugarcane has proved a decided success.

As an agricultural centre for this part of Arizona, Florence bears the palm. But Florence is also our county seat, and with its fine Court-house, polite and accommodating officials, good hotels and pleasant society—it invites the gathering litigants, jurors and witnesses to its semi-annual court terms, and also to a pleasant stay and recreation from their usual avocations during the sessions of court.

The rich mineral region surrounding this smiling, quiet town or nearly every side—has for years sought Florence as its place of supplies, and "the start" for many presently promising mining camps has been Florence. Its enterprising merchants and business men will not, in the rapid growth of all around them, be behind in the race of progress and development. Let us know but one aim for the exertion of our energies—let our efforts be united in the grand enterprise of developing our virgin territory, and let us go hand in hand on the march towards greatness, wealth and happiness.

The New Mining Law.

Our delegate in Congress, the Hon John G. Campbell, has forwarded us a copy of the amendments to the Act of May 10th, 1872, which concerns all prospectors and owners of mining claims, and reads as follows:

An Act to amend Sections twenty-three hundred and twenty four and twenty three hundred and twenty-five of the Revised Statutes of the United States concerning mineral lands.

Be it enacted by the Senate and House of Representatives of the United States of America in Congress assembled, that section twenty-three hundred and twenty-five of the Revised Statutes of the United States be amended by adding thereto the following words: "Provided, That where the claimant for a patent is not a resident of or within the land district wherein the vein, lode, ledge, or deposit sought to be patented is located, the application for patent and the affidavits required to be made in this section by the claimant for such patent may be made by his, her, or its authorized agent, where said agent is conversant with the facts sought to be established by said affidavits: And provided that this section shall apply to all applications now pending for patents to mineral lands."

Sec. 2. That section twenty three hundred and twenty-four of the Revised Statutes of the United States be amended by adding the following words: "Provided, That the period within which the work required to be done annually on all unpatented mineral claims shall commence on the first day of January succeeding the date of location of each claim, and this section shall apply to all claims located since the 10th day of May, A. D. 1872."

Approved January 22d, 1880.

"Dear friend Huntley," who cuts all. Backers clothes, at No. 66 Wabash avenue, Chicago, writes us affectionately, that he has been "in clothes" for the last fifteen years. Now, friend Huntley, please take your clothes off when you go to bed, advertise largely in our paper, and get rich. Lots of folks here would like to have your clothes if they are not too old.

In response to a fond mother's query: "How are you, dear boy!" the dear boy writes back from Leadville: "I am pretty well, mother; getting along first-rate. Have gained twenty pounds since I have been here, in half ounce installments. Have not yet been shot in the head."

119
P

Above—Pinal, *circa* 1885. Ore teams from the Silver King Mine at the mills in Pinal. The teams made one round trip of twelve miles a day.—*Courtesy Arizona Pioneers' Historical Society*

Martin's Blacksmith Shop, Pinal, 1882.—*Courtesy Arizona Pioneers' Historical Society*

Pioneer

COUNTY: *Gila*
LOCATION: *15 mi. southwest of Globe*
MAP: *page 191*
P.O. est. as Pioneer, April 24, 1882; discont. Sept. 4, 1885.

Pioneer was the result of silver mines located about 1877. The leading mines were the Pioneer, South Pioneer, and Howard. Blessed with abundant wood, water, and high-grade ores, Pioneer quickly developed into a lively mining camp. A good school, brewery, bank, hotel, general stores, sawmill, and extensive reduction works were some of Pioneer's assets. About four hundred men worked at the mill and mines.

The camp did not last long. Apparently, the Howard Mining Company of Cleveland, Ohio, which operated the twenty-stamp mill was not successful. About 1885 the mill shut down, and two years later it was destroyed by fire.

A ranch is now situated at Pioneer, but some old foundations of the former town are still visible.

Placerita

COUNTY: *Yavapai*
LOCATION: *about 20 mi. south of Prescott*
MAP: *page 189*
P.O. est. as Placerita, Feb. 1, 1896; discont. Aug. 15, 1910.

Gold placers along Placerita Gulch had been known and worked for years prior to the establishment of the post office and camp. In addition to mining, Placerita also subsisted on goat and cattle ranching. A population of thirty was reported in 1905.

About three buildings and extensive rubble are left, scattered along the gulch.

Abandoned rock house at Placerita.

Placerita — wooden building and bedstead.

Home of a prospector, date unknown.—
Courtesy Sharlot Hall Museum

Planet and Eagle Landing

PLANET—COUNTY: *Yuma*
LOCATION: *about 10 mi. east of Parker Dam on Bill Williams River*
MAP: *page 177*
P.O. est. as Planet, March 28, 1902; discont. March 31, 1921.
EAGLE LANDING—COUNTY: *Yuma*
LOCATION: *6 mi. northeast of Parker*
MAP: *page 177*
P.O. none.

Richard Ryland discovered the Planet copper mine in 1863. It was the second copper mine discovered and worked by Americans in Arizona. With the establishment of the Planet Copper Company, work began and the community of Planet took form around the mining activity. It was not a large place—there were a post office, a couple of general merchandise stores, a few other business concerns, and several private dwellings. For years the mine produced. Then, in 1917, it closed. Since there was no other employment, miners left and Planet shriveled into a ghost town.

Eagle Landing served as a shipping point for ore from the Planet Mine. Located on the Colorado River some fifteen miles west of Planet, the landing seems to have been rather an insignificant place.

Poland

COUNTY: *Yavapai*
LOCATION: *9 mi. southeast of Prescott*
MAP: *page 189*
P.O. est. as Poland, Nov. 16, 1901; discont. Feb. 15, 1913.

At the turn of the century an embryo camp was growing on upper Big Bug Creek. Known as Poland, the small mountain burg owed its name to Davis Robert Poland (b. Tennessee, 1834; d. February 23, 1882), who arrived in Arizona in 1864. Eight years later he discovered the Poland Mine.

By 1902 the settlement of Poland had matured into an active mining town. A post office had opened, a fine lodginghouse of fourteen rooms had just been completed, a general store was thriving, and the future looked promising. In a few more years, Poland blossomed into a community of eight hundred people, half a dozen saloons, stores, a school, several boardinghouses, and the South Poland Hotel.

As ore began to wane, a tunnel was cut through the mountain to the town of Walker, a distance of about two miles. The purpose of the tunnel was further exploration, but it was also a great asset to Walker. Ore from the Sheldon Mine at Walker could be hauled by mule train through the tunnel and shipped out by a branch line of the Prescott-Crown King Railroad, which joined the main line five miles from the tunnel at Poland Junction.

A miner's life was long hours and poor pay. In 1901 mine employees at Poland worked seven days a week for a daily stipend of $2.25. This amount did not include food and lodging, which cost $1.00 a day. The miners did not complain until 1905, when they struck for higher wages. They wanted a daily increase of $.25. Gradually salaries improved, but never by a large amount. The eight men who worked a twelve-hour shift in Poland's twenty-stamp mill received a meager $4.00 a day.

There was some ore production during the 1920's and 1930's, but for all practical purposes not enough to keep Poland alive. The inevitable exodus took place.

In recent years, summer cottages and homes have occupied the site of Poland.

View of Poland, 1904, looking west.—*Courtesy Shar-lot Hall Museum*

Poland, 1905 — South Po-land Hotel and Saloon.—*Courtesy Sharlot Hall Mu-seum*

Polaris

COUNTY: *Yuma*
LOCATION: *about 37 mi. southeast of Quartzsite*
MAP: *page 179*
P.O. est. as Polaris, June 17, 1909; discont. July 31, 1914.

In the 1890's, Felix Mayhew was employed at the King of Arizona Mine, working the night shift. During the day, when not sleeping, he managed to do a little prospecting. On one excursion, Mayhew discovered a promising ledge about two miles from the King. A man at the King of Arizona known as the "Expert" proclaimed the vein worthless, but Mayhew persisted. He staked a claim, and then in 1907 sold his prospect, the North Star Gold Mine, to the Golden Star Mining Company for $350,000.

Polaris, the mining camp for the North Star, included the typical hard-working miners, the usual businesses, and a reported 150 residences.

Mining was profitable until 1911. When the ore vein reached its economical limits, the mine closed and Polaris succumbed.

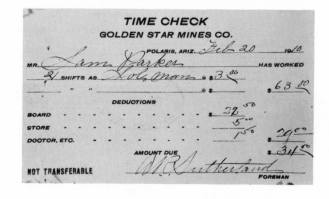

Polaris, 1910.—*Courtesy Yuma County Historical Society*

Polaris, 1910, meal ticket.—*Courtesy Yuma County Historical Society*

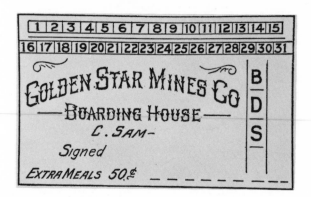

Polaris, *circa* 1900. Owners of the North Star Mine, left to right: top row, Sam DeCorse, Nick Larsen, Charles DeCorse; bottom row, Juan Verdugo, Felix Mayhew, Bill Smith.—*Courtesy Yuma Territorial Prison Museum*

Polaris, *circa* 1900.—*Courtesy Yuma County Historical Society*

Polhamus Landing

COUNTY: *Mohave*
LOCATION: *near present site of Davis Dam*
MAP: *page 175*
P.O. none.

Captain Polhamus was not a greenhorn when he began navigating steamers on the Colorado River. As a boy he had worked for his father as a pilot on the Hudson River. Born in New York City in 1828, Isaac Polhamus left his native terrain and sailed for San Francisco in 1846. For a number of years he worked for one of the steamboat companies running on the Sacramento River. Then, in 1856, he was hired by the Colorado Steam Navigation Company and went to Yuma. In those early days, Yuma was only a small landing place containing the company office, but it was good enough for Polhamus. He lived in Yuma for sixty-six years and died there in 1922, at the age of ninety-four.

Navigating paddle-wheelers on the treacherous Colorado required the utmost skill and courage. Captain Polhamus had more than the necessary qualities of an expert navigator. He eventually rose to the rank of general superintendent of the navigation company's fleet.

In 1881 a new river landing was established five miles above Hardyville and named in honor of the greatly-respected Captain Polhamus. It consisted of a large warehouse and a scattering of other buildings. Here freight was landed for various interior points.

Like all the other Colorado River ports, Polhamus Landing became obsolete when railroads took over.

Yuma, *circa* 1870's—office of Colorado Steam Navigation Co. Captain Issac Polhamus (1828–1922), second man from the right.—*Courtesy University of Arizona, Special Collections*

Queen

COUNTY: *Pinal*
LOCATION: *present site of Superior at mouth of Queen Creek Canyon*
MAP: *page 191*
P.O. est. as Queen, April 21, 1881; discont. Sept. 5, 1881.

Situated at the mouth of Queen Creek Canyon, this short-lived camp is now the present site of Superior. Occupied mostly by miners in the early 1880's, Queen contained about a hundred inhabitants, a general store, saloons, a boardinghouse, a restaurant, and two hotels—a total of twenty buildings and a number of tents. An important feature was the Gem Mill.

The historic bluff over which a band of Apaches leaped to their death while being pursued by General Crook's troops in the 1870's towers above the site of Queen. Human skulls and bones resulting from this mass annihilation could be found by residents of the camp in the early 1880's.

Queen, anticipating the future importance of its location, predicted that Queen Creek Canyon would someday become a main thoroughfare. Today a highway winds up the canyon, linking Globe and Superior, but Queen has long since vanished.

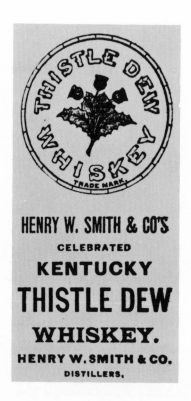

Advertisements from the Pinal newspaper *The Drill,* 1881. These advertisements were typical of the period.—*Courtesy Arizona Pioneers' Historical Society*

Quijotoa

COUNTY: *Pima*
LOCATION: *20 mi. northwest of Sells*
MAP: *page 185*
P.O. est. as Quijotoa, Dec. 11, 1883; discont. Aug. 31, 1942.

Alexander McKay discovered an outcrop at the summit of Ben Nevis Mountain in 1883. Containing copper and silver, the deposit looked good. News spread rapidly, soon reaching the attention of San Francisco speculators, who sent mining experts to look over the alleged bonanza. The result was that half a dozen mining companies were formed immediately.

Following the mine discovery, two brothers, J. T. and W. R. Logan, began digging a well on the east side of Ben Nevis Mountain. At the well, a small camp which began to grow became known as the Logan townsite. Meanwhile, the adjoining rival townsite of New Virginia was beginning to develop.

By 1884 Logan Avenue, which emerged into Main Street, New Virginia, embraced a row of one-story wooden buildings and adobes three-fourths of a mile long. With the addition of two more adjoining townsites, Virginia City and Brooklyn, the camp included some two hundred buildings.

Quijotoa was a composite of all four townsites, and the Quijotoa post office was located in New Virginia. The cost of living was not high in Quijotoa. The price of meals varied between twenty-five and fifty cents, and drinks cost twelve and a half cents. Water was brought from Covered Wells and Allen, Papago Indians supplied milk and hay, and wood and wild game were abundant. Added to these attributes were two daily stage lines running between Tucson and Quijotoa, and business concerns of every kind and description.

Despite the fact that there were some twenty saloons, Quijotoa maintained fairly good law and order. There was no jail, but Thomas D. Casanega, deputy sheriff, solved that problem by merely tying prisoners to a tree under which cots were placed. The next morning, the offenders would be shipped out on the departing stage for Tucson.

Arriving at Quijotoa in February, 1884, was Harry Brook, formerly connected with the *Pinal Drill* and *San Francisco Wasp* newspapers. In two hours he took in $250 in subscriptions to the forthcoming camp newspaper. The first copy of *The Prospector,* consisting of four pages, came out on February 16, 1884.

Harry Newton, owner of a large corral at Quijotoa, had a Winchester, upon the shooting qualities of which he was always ready to bet his last penny. One day Toppy Johnson, a local resident, decided to have a little fun with Harry. Toppy, out hunting, killed a coyote. Bringing the animal's carcass back to Quijotoa, he propped it up against a cactus about a hundred yards from Harry's tent. Then he pulled aside the tent flap and asked Harry to lend him a gun because there was a coyote outside he wanted to kill. Harry jumped at the bait. He insisted on proving to Toppy that he could kill the coyote with one shot, even betting Toppy $40 that he could do it. Harry took careful aim and fired. The coyote did not budge. Certain that he could hit his prey on the second try, Harry bet Toppy $100 more. Again his shot failed to arouse the coyote. Toppy quietly pocketed his $140 as Harry furiously started for the coyote, determined to kill the critter that had just cost him so much money. Before he knew it, Harry had walked straight up to the coyote. Turning over the dead animal he caught sight of the third bullet hole and realized he had been victimized. Meanwhile, Toppy explained the joke to the boys. All had a good laugh on Harry; then Toppy fled.

The ore deposit did not prove to be the rich bonanza expected. Harry Brook packed up and moved his printing outfit to Tucson in the fall of 1884. Others began to leave. Quijotoa was well into a decline when a fire broke out about noon on June 26, 1889. Starting in Archie Nivens' building on Main Street, the blaze nearly reduced the town to ashes. There was no reason to rebuild.

A population of several thousand people and four townsites had tapered to sixty people and a dilapidated camp by 1891. Today the encroaching desert has swallowed up all trace of ruins.

THE PROSPECTOR.

VOLUME I. | QUIJOTOA, A. T. FEBRUARY 16, 1884. | NUMBER 1.

THE PROSPECTOR.

SATURDAY · FEBRUARY 16, 1884.

PUBLISHED WEEKLY
BY
HARRY BROOK,
EDITOR AND PROPRIETOR.
QUIJOTOA, ARIZONA.

RATES OF SUBSCRIPTION.

One year.....................$5.00.
Six months.....................3.00.

PAYABLE IN ADVANCE.

Single Copies 15 cents.
Copies may be had at J. S. Mansfeld's Book Store, Quijotoa.

KINLEY, FERGUSON & WALSH.
ATTORNEYS AT LAW.
213 CONGRESS STREET, TUCSON, A. T.

The Dollar.

"Thou dollar of our respected ancestors! Our acknowledged governor, preserver and benefactor. Without thee in the world we could do nothing; but with thee we can do all things. When the rheumatism lays its palsying hand upon us, thou canst provide the tenderest nurses, the most skillful physicians or a ticket to the hot springs; when our [illegible]es have assumed a horizontal attitude, and we are planted 'neath the daisies, and a tombstone with a lying epitaph, thou canst provide a brass band of sixteen pieces and a $4,000 hearse. Thou canst fee lawyers and bribe juries; adorn the gentleman and the jackass; thou art the joy of our youth and the solace of our old age. Thou, almighty dollar, art worshiped the world over. Thou art the favorite of the old fool and the philosopher; thou hast no hypocrites in thy temples, nor false heart at thy altars; thou art loved by the civilized and the savage with unfeigned and unfaltering affection. Thou hast placed armies in the field, and navies upon the ocean, and at the uplifting of thy powerful hand their thunders break forth and their lightnings flash. Thou art the awakener of our energies, the guide of our footsteps, the goal of our being, the handmaiden of our religion and the twin sister of charity. O, almighty dollar, be with us we beseech thee, attended by an inexpressible number of thy ministering angels made in thine own image. Permit us to possess thee in abundance—such abundance indeed, that thy gladdening light shall illumine the vale of penury and want like a 2000 candle power electric light, and cause my awakened soul to break forth in acclamations of joy."—Laramie Boomerang.

Too Late.

It appeared to be a private confab, as the two men sat with their backs to the iron fence of the Trinity church.

"If you was Jay Gould," said one, "and I was a Judge on the Bench, how much would you give to own me?"

"Well, I dunno," "How much would you take?"

"Make me an offer."

"Well, I'd chip in with Jim Keene and Russell Sage and Uncle Rufus, and I reckon we'd offer you $20,000.

"Hoot! toot! man, but you'd get left! While you were getting up the pool President Villard would step in with an offer of $25,000."

Verdict for Plaintiff.—Wall Street News.

A skeleton has been found in a cave in Arkansas. The skeleton and surroundings indicate antiquity, and it is thought the cave is in close proximity to silver mines, which, according to a legend, are reported to have been worked by Spaniards, and all traces effectually closed.

The judgment of the Schieffelin brothers that the season in Alaska is too short to render mining profitable, is no doubt correct, except in the case of such mammoth ledges as the Treadwell. Returning miners bring many samples of fine coal and a superior quality of white marble.—[West Shore.

QUIJOTOA.

Its Past, Present and Future.

Where Quijotoa now stands there were, on the first of January, a couple of tents. All around was a dry and deserted land, no water within ten miles. There are now a mile of houses, and a population, in and around the camp, of at least 1200.

The happy discovery of the wonderful mines on the summit of Quijotoa mountain has drawn the eyes of the whole Pacific Coast to this spot. It is true, that the subsequent purchase of these mines by Flood & Co. gave an impetus to the excitement, which it would not have received had the purchasers been unknown parties. There is, however, much reason in this, for the bonanza firm are known to be experienced mining men, who mean business, and do nothing on a small scale. We know that there will be none of that miserable inefficiency of management which has cursed so many of our mines.

We are now waiting for the cutting of the ledge in the tunnels which are being run. That they will find the ore go down, there is hardly any doubt in the minds of the many experienced mining men who have visited the ground. Quijotoa will then take her real start. We have a most glorious climate, superior to that which any prominent mining camp on this coast can show. No snows or frosts to impede work of all descriptions, which can be carried on in the open air the year round. The opening of 1885 will see a city here, compared with which Tombstone, Virginia City and Leadville are mere villages.

FLOAT.

It is proposed to organize a tender-[illegible] foot society, to include all who came to the Territory previous to 1885.

There is a heavy dew on the ground in the morning at Quijotoa, something unusual in Arizona. The fact that it is not over seventy miles, in an air line, to the gulf, will probably account for the phenomenon.

Every business is represented here, except a pawnbroker, and every nation, except China.

It is expected that the telegraph line from Tucson will be working by March 1st. The rate will be fifty cents for ten words, and four cents a word after that.

Fire insurance costs ten per cent.

It would be a good idea to have our lumber houses painted with fire proof paint.

We are a quiet and law abiding community and propose to remain so. Rowdies will find this an unhealthy camp.

There will soon be enough "specimens" in town to start up a five stamp mill.

Quijotoa wants a railroad depot, an opera house and a bank.

The town-site of Logan was taken up first as a homestead, and the mineral ground thereon then covered by mining claims, so that there can be no question of title.

It costs ten dollars to be a Pioneer.

Lots in Logan are not sold, but leased for 99 years.

Where We Are.

Quijotoa, comprising the towns of Logan and New Virginia, now practically one, and their suburbs, is situated in Pima county, 65 miles west of Tucson and about the same distance south of Casa Grande, on the S. P. R. R. The town is built on a sloping bench of land which connects the mesa with the bonanza mountain on the east. The situation is very healthy, the ground being hard and the gradual fall allowing of a perfect drainage. In fact, a more healthy location can hardly be imagined. A mile of houses, many of them large handsome buildings of lumber, extends along the main street—Logan Avenue—and through New Virginia, on the East. The ground on the North and South of the main street is a little broken and will need some grading. The townsites are covered with a growth of palo verde, cactus and some mesquite bushes, which are being rapidly cleared off.

WONDERFUL.

Pioneer Date Guage.

A serious question has arisen in the Pioneer Society as to the best means of verifying the asserted date of arrival of the various members. The great majority of the hardy old settlers are perfect George Washingtons, but it is feared that here and there a dishonorable soul, contaminated by too much contact with tenderfeet, may endeavor to obtain membership without having been in the country sufficiently long enough to qualify. How to obviate this danger has been a burning question, and a most ingenious expedient has now been hit upon.

It is well known among close observers that a lengthened residence in this Territory is conducive to mental aberration, or, to put it plainly, to insanity. Whether this is owing to the extremely dry air, the hardness of the water, or the quality of the whisky, is as yet undetermined, the fact remains the same. It is only a matter of time 'ere the old resident becomes a boarder at that elegant brick building in San Joaquin county, California, which is chiefly supported by our contingent funds. This being the case, it is proposed to engage a leading specialist, who has made a life long study of cerebral idiosyncrasies, as official expert of the society. His duty will be to examine the brains of all candidates for admission, in order to determine the date of their arrival, and he expects to establish a guage which will indicate to within three months the day when the applicant first set foot in the Territory. The advances in the field of scientific investigation are truly wonderful.

The cattle business [illegible] year will see a boom it has never known before, the expressed doubts of the weak kneed and pessimists to the contrary notwithstanding, and the bright shekels will be gathered in by stockmen at a rate before unknown. All of the straws and all of the saw-logs, up to the present time, point unmistakably that way. The mild winters throughout the southwest, coupled with the favorable reports from the market centers and the new ranges being opened up, have had the effect of raising the prices of ranges, giving them a degree of stiffness to at least hold to the raise, and the season now almost here will see well established range property hard to get hold of at prices enhanced from those of last year. Owing to the unfavorable condition for fattening on the range the past year a less per centage than ordinarily was shipped and immense gains will be made by the steers in the added year, and the beef output promises to be greater than for several years; which is met by a healthy and constantly increasing demand on the part of consumers. The most favorable conditions obtained all over the range countries after it was generally considered unsafe to ship, owing to the advanced season, and these seasons continue without a break up to the present month, and in the Panhandle and the ranges south experiencing no serious reverses even yet. With a reasonably favorable spring, returns will be coming to the ranges early in the season, and will be heavy. At no time in the history of the business has the outlook for stockmen ever been so golden as now, over the range country as a whole.—[Live Stock Journal.

The first profile taken of which there is any record is that of Antigonus, who had but one eye. This likeness was taken in 330 B. C. Addison says that until the close of the third century the Roman Emperors were always painted in profile, which position was thought to give a very majestic view of the head.

It is claimed by experts in the cattle business that the entire expense of raising a steer up to four years of age is about $1.80 in this Territory and New Mexico. A four-year old steer in good condition is worth $35.

A Kansas Justice of the Peace has reduced his matrimonial business to a very brief and concise formula. This is the ceremony: "Have 'er?" "Yes." "Have 'im?" "Yes." "Married, $2.00."

"It is passing strange," resumed the philosopher, "that so many people have died during the last decade, and yet so few of them come back." Then his wife hit him over the ear with a hassock and told him to go down to the grocery and get some red herrings for breakfast.

Farmers on Salt river and Tonto, in this county, have about completed seeding. In some places grain is up and looks well.

The Grand Army of the Republic has now on its rolls a quarter of a million members in good standing.

Quacks.

The ancient highwayman was a considerate person. His demands might sometimes seem urgent, but they kept within certain bounds. He gave you a choice of evils. If you would surrender your money you might keep your life, and doubtless he often praised himself for easing you of that which might have proved to you a snare while he granted you the most precious of earthly blessings.

The modern quack doctor is a much more bloodthirsty character. He has no such scruples as the highwayman, and no such moderation in his demands. With him there is no alternative. He wants your money and your life. When he has got your money he goes on to deprive you of your life. He makes you pay him heavily for putting you to death.

Precisely how large is the addition made by these blood-suckers to our bills of mortality will never be known until the judgment day. And it would be difficult, no doubt, to estimate the amount of money that they annually extort from their victims. Those who have some means of knowing the condition and the habits of the humbler classes are aware that the amount is very large. It is a pity that the facts cannot be brought to light. Will not General Walker try to include this item in the tables of the next census? If it were only known how much these people are doing to impoverish and destroy human beings, a society with a longer name than of Bergh's would soon arise for their suppression.—Good Company.

[illegible]

A good story is told of the well known engineer, William A. Sweet, of Syracuse. Casually meeting a prominent lawyer one day, a brief conversation ensued, in the course of which Mr. Sweet happened to ask "the judge" what he thought of some questions they were discussing, without really meaning to ask legal advice in the usual way. Soon afterward Mr. Sweet received a bill from the judge "for legal advice, $1,000," which he paid promptly without a word or complaint.

Time passed on, and one day the judge, who was also heavily interested in salt manufacture, needed some mechanical advice about machinery which was not running satisfactorily, and asked Mr. Sweet to look at the machines and tell him what was needed. Mr. Sweet looked them over for two or three hours, and indicated the cause of the trouble. When he went home he promptly made a bill out against the judge for "mechanical advice, $1,500," and the bill was duly paid, furnishing probably one of the few instances on record in which mechanics ever get ahead of the law.—American Machinest.

Willing to Accommodate.

A gentleman who yesterday appeared at the Eastern Haymarket in search of fodder for his horse was at once surrounded by a half dozen owners of loads anxious to sell. When they had exhausted their breath in shouting "timothy," he quietly replied:

"All your loads look fine enough but I'm a little particular."

"Why—how—what!" they shouted,

"I want a load of hay with about one hundred and fifty pounds of stones in the center of it."

All fell back with injured looks upon their faces, but presently one seller gave the gentleman a wink to cross the street to a saloon. When both were out of sight of the crowd he whispered:

"Say, I've got the load you want."

"Are the rocks there?"

"No, but my son William is lying alongside the binder under that blanket. He won't quite pull down 150 pounds, but I'll steal you four or five sticks of good cord wood to make up the difference."—[Detroit Free Press.

Idaho is somewhat alarmed at the encroachment of the Mormons upon the most fertile portions of her territory. We ought to settle this Mormon business,

Quijotoa, 1884—first page of first edition of *The Prospector.—Courtesy Arizona Pioneers' Historical Society*

Reymert

COUNTY: *Pinal*
LOCATION: *about 11 mi. southwest of Superior*
MAP: *page 191*
P.O. *est. as Reymert, June 6, 1890; discont. May 27, 1898.*

A mine some eighteen miles northeast of Florence was relocated about 1880 by James DeNoon Reymert, who subsequently gave his name to the mine and resulting camp.

Reymert, a native of Norway, came to America and settled in Arizona Territory about 1876. He opened a law office, edited the *Pinal Drill* newspaper and founded the camp of DeNoon.

In 1889 Reymert camp was busily employing seventy-five men who were working the mine, grading roads, and erecting buildings.

Although the Reymert post office closed in the late 1890's, work continued at the mine until 1950. Today there are fourteen or fifteen deserted buildings at the site.

Richinbar

COUNTY: *Yavapai*
LOCATION: *4 mi. east of Bumble Bee*
MAP: *page 189*
P.O. *est. as Richinbar, July 30, 1896; discont. March 15, 1912.*

The Richinbar gold mine supported a small camp of the same name. During the life of the Richinbar post office, the population probably did not exceed fifty. Duquesne Mining Company and Kentucky Standard Mining Company operated here.

The site of the Reymert Mine, producer of some $500,000 worth of silver between 1887 and 1930. There is some question whether this location was called DeNoon or Reymert.

Rosemont

COUNTY: *Pima*
LOCATION: *12 mi. north of Sonoita*
MAP: *page 195*
P.O. est. as Rosemont, Sept. 27, 1894; discont. May 31, 1910.

L. J. Rose and William B. McCleary located an extensive group of copper mines in the late 1870's or early 1880's. The claims were incorporated under the name Rosemont Smelting and Mining Company. The two owners ran heavily into debt, so they finally sold the mining property to the Lewisohn brothers of New York City, who did considerable work and then shut down.

Rosemont camp developed near the smelter and supported about 150 residents, a school, a hotel, and some stores. After the closing of the mines and smelter, Rosemont was deserted. Nothing is left today.

Ruby

COUNTY: *Santa Cruz*
LOCATION: *about 30 mi. northwest of Nogales*
MAP: *page 195*
P.O. est. as Ruby, April 11, 1912; discont. May 31, 1941.

In the post–Civil War years, extensive prospecting in the Oro Blanco district led to the discovery of the rich Montana Mine in the 1870's. A jumble of cabins, shacks, and tents grew into Montana camp. For approximately forty years the camp retained its original name. In 1909, when mining accelerated, Julius Andrews, who was in charge of the camp store, made an application for a post office. His request was granted. On April 11, 1912, the post office was established as Ruby, in honor of Lillie B. Ruby, Andrews' wife.

Philip M. Clarke purchased Andrews' store and post office in 1913 and proceeded to construct another combination store and post office on top of a hill some four hundred yards north of the old building. Maybe there was some truth to the Mexican superstition that the store was cursed because it was built over a padre's grave. Before many years had elapsed, the new building was the scene of two savage and inhuman attacks.

Two brothers, Alex and John Frazier, were hired by Clarke to act as storekeeper and postmaster. One day in February, 1920, a Mexican ranch hand stopped at the store. Finding the door locked and his knocks not answered, he looked through the window. There on the floor lay the brothers, with the safe wide open and the only telephone in Ruby ripped from the wall. The horrified Mexican jumped on his horse and raced to the ranch of John Mahoney, justice of the peace. Sheriff Earhart and an ambulance were sent for, from Nogales. Arriving at the scene of the crime, Earhart found Alex dead and John unconscious. John died without regaining consciousness. Months of investigation failed to produce any positive clues as to the identity of the murderer or murderers.

The second attack took place a year later when Frank Pearson and his wife Myrtle had taken over the running of the store. Pearson's sister Irene and his sister-in-law Elizabeth Purcell were visiting them at the time and helping Myrtle with her tasks. On a hot August day in 1921, several vaqueros arrived at the store and asked for tobacco. As Frank turned to get it, a gunshot rang out and Pearson fell dead. In the confusion that followed, Elizabeth, grazed by a bullet, fainted; Irene escaped with the Pearson's four-year-old daughter; and Myrtle was shot. As she lay dying, one of the murderers spied her five gold front teeth and with the butt of his gun brutally knocked them out and pocketed them. After looting the safe, the gang fled across the border.

There followed a most extensive and thorough search. A posse took up the outlaws' trail, an airplane—the first ever used in Arizona for a manhunt—flew over the area, and a reward of $5,000 was offered for each of the murderers, dead or alive.

In April of 1922 a deputy overheard a bartender in a cantina in Sasabe, Sonora, trying to sell five gold teeth to a customer. When questioned by the deputy, the bartender revealed that he had obtained the teeth from Manuel Martinez. In short order, Martinez and his companion in crime,

Placido Silvas, were arrested and positively identified as the murderers. Martinez was sentenced to death and Silvas to life imprisonment. While the prisoners were being driven to the state penitentiary at Florence by Deputies White and Smith, the car careened off the road and overturned, killing White and injuring Smith. The outlaws escaped, but were recaptured six days later. Martinez kept his scheduled date with death on August 10, 1923.

After the Eagle Picher Company of Saint Louis purchased the ten Montana claims in 1927, continued expansion and development of the mine sent Ruby into a new era of prosperity. People poured into camp, erecting houses and establishing businesses. Some 300 men were employed by the Montana Mine and almost 150 children attended the new four-room school. In 1941 the Eagle Picher Company ended operations at Ruby. Since then it has been a ghost town.

Placido Silvas, 1922.—*Courtesy Arizona Pioneers' Historical Society*

Manuel Martinez, 1922.—*Courtesy Arizona Pioneers' Historical Society*

Above—Ruby—deserted store and post office where murders occurred.

Right—Ruby, 1938.—*Courtesy Arizona Pioneers' Historical Society*

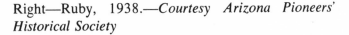

Present-day Ruby, looking south toward the Mexican border and Montana Peak at the left.

Russellville

COUNTY: *Cochise*
LOCATION: *17 mi. southwest of Willcox*
MAP: *page 195*
P.O. *none.*

The Peabody Mine was owned by the Russell Gold & Silver Mining Company. At the site of the mine smelter, Russellville sprang into existence about 1881. Composed of approximately a hundred souls, the camp was reported to be prosperous and thrifty. The presence of women and families lent an air of refinement to the orderly and law-abiding community. Through the efforts of enterprising businessmen and merchants, Russellville acquired facilities for cheap and comfortable living. A general store, a blacksmith shop, saloons, and restaurants formed the business district. Dragoon served as the camp's post office and general communications contact with the outside world.

One day in June of 1882, quite a scare was created when several Indians passed by Russellville. As it turned out, they were peaceable Indian scouts employed by the government. Consequently, a request was made that white men ride with the scouts when they roamed the country, otherwise, the Indians might be shot by mistake.

The town of Johnson, established nearer the Peabody Mine in 1883, stole Russellville's residents. A mass movement to the new settlement left Russellville abandoned.

Salero

COUNTY: *Santa Cruz*
LOCATION: *about 18 mi. northeast of Nogales*
MAP: *page 195*
P.O. est. as Salero, Aug. 13, 1884; discont. April 17, 1890.

Under the direction of the Jesuits, Mexicans first worked the Salero Mine in the eighteenth century. A tale is told of the derivation of the name Salero, meaning saltcellar, which supposedly originated sometime during these early years of the mine's history. The priests at Tumacacori, expecting a visit from the Bishop of Sonora, planned a most sumptuous feast in his honor. Being somewhat a *bon vivant,* the good bishop appeared delighted with the excellent chicken, fruit, and wine assiduously laid before him. Only one luxury was lacking—a saltcellar. The padre in charge, deeply mortified at his oversight, immediately dispatched a few men to the Santa Rita Mountains with orders to mine some native silver and fashion a saltcellar. The saltcellar was made, and the mine which supplied the silver received its name.

In 1857 the Salero Mining Company of Cincinnati, Ohio, acquired the mine property. Headed by John Wrightson, manager; H. C. Grosvenor, engineer; Gilbert W. Hopkins, mineralogist; and Raphael Pumpelly, engineer, the company had its headquarters at Tubac. All these men, with the exception of Pumpelly, were later killed by Apaches.

The relocation of the Salero Mine in the 1870's by George Clark produced a mining community that warranted a post office.

The silver mining camp of Salero on the southwest slope of the Santa Rita Mountains, 1909. —*Courtesy Arizona Pioneers' Historical Society*

Sasco—present-day ruins.

Sasco

COUNTY: *Pinal*
LOCATION: *about 15 mi. southwest of Red Rock*
MAP: *page 185*
P.O. est. as Sasco, July 10, 1907; discont. Sept. 15, 1919.

Sasco (Southern Arizona Smelting Company), a smelter town, processed ore from the Silver Bell Mine and the Picacho Mining Company mines. Founded in the early years of the present century, Sasco was a prosperous place until 1910, when the furnaces closed because of insufficient profit. During Sasco's heyday, 600 people lived in the town, and some 175 men were on the company payroll. There were the usual stores, saloons, and lodging facilities. A daily train on the Arizona Southern Railroad ran between Red Rock and Silverbell, providing transportation for Sasco residents.

A murder occurred at Sasco in April of 1919. Charley Coleman, a man of questionable reputation, arrived in Sasco from Bisbee with the announced intention of killing two men. Apparently Mrs. Coleman, who lived in Sasco, renting a room in the saloon building owned by Mr. Wilson, had attracted the attention of male admirers. Although Coleman was not in Sasco, he somehow learned of the fact and decided to do away with two of his wife's suitors. After jumping from a moving train as it pulled through Red Rock, Coleman hired a horse and rode into the smelter town. Before encountering his intended victims, he called on his wife in her room. When an argument between the two began to cause considerable disturbance, Mr. Wilson, the saloon owner, interfered and ordered Coleman to leave. Coleman refused, so Wilson left the room, went into his saloon, and immediately returned with a thirty-thirty rifle. Without hesitating, he shot and killed Coleman. At the time of his death, Coleman was in the process of setting a trap for his victims. He had been in the act of compelling one of the saloon women to write letters to his wife's admirers asking them to call on Mrs. Coleman because she wished to see them.

Foundations of a smelting furnace, a substantial stone building, a concrete building, foundations, broken glass, and rusty cans are scattered over the deserted townsite.

Senator

COUNTY: *Yavapai*
LOCATION: *about 11 mi. south of Prescott*
MAP: *page 189*
P.O. est. as Senator, Nov. 1, 1915; discont. Oct. 22, 1918.

The Senator gold mine, discovered in the late 1860's, gave rise to a community of the same name. From 1883 to 1899 the mine was worked by various miners and then by Phelps Dodge. Enough families resided at Senator to warrant having a school.

The mine lay idle from 1899 to 1915, when lessees took over. Senator camp revived at that time and supported a post office for several years.

Sasco—concrete foundations of the smelting furnace complex.

Senator, *circa* 1883.—*Courtesy Sharlot Hall Museum*

ment for the occupants of Seymour. Situated on the opposite side of the river from the stamp mill, the small town had one principal street, a score of buildings, and a fluctuating but fairly large population. One of Seymour's business enterprises was a Chinese laundry operated by Yellow Dick, once "Mayor" of Phoenix Chinatown.

The mill ran for about a year. Then in 1879–80 it was dismantled and the parts used to construct another mill at the Vulture Mine. Seymour was finished as a milling community. Since there was no longer a means of making a livelihood, people scattered.

When the Central Arizona Mining Company moved the mill to Vulture, there was a water problem to solve. Consequently, a pipeline was laid from the Hassayampa River, where a pumping plant was installed on the west bank, to the mine. At the plant the few remaining hangers-on of the defunct milling town gathered. Here Seymour Station, a corral, and a store were kept by Danny Conger and a mercantile establishment by S. Michaels. For the most part, the other residents were employees of the Vulture, who attended to the pumping plant.

In 1917 one old building marked the townsite of Seymour.

Seymour

COUNTY: *Maricopa*
LOCATION: *10 mi. south of Wickenburg*
MAP: *page 183*
P.O. est. as Seymour, June 20, 1879; discont. sometime after midsummer, 1883.

After James Seymour of New York obtained possession of the Vulture Mine for the Central Arizona Mining Company in 1878, a twenty-stamp mill was erected on the Hassayampa River, ten miles from Vulture. The mill provided employ-

Signal and Liverpool Landing

SIGNAL—COUNTY: *Mohave*
LOCATION: *22 mi. south of Wikieup*
MAP: *page 177*
P.O. est. as Signal, Oct. 15, 1877; discont. May 14, 1932.
LIVERPOOL LANDING—COUNTY: *Mohave*
LOCATION: *about 20 mi. north of Parker Dam*
MAP: *page 177*
P.O. none.

The discovery of the McCracken silver mine in 1874 generated excitement in mining circles and produced the inevitable rush to the newly-formed Owens district. Signal burst into life about 1877, as the mills for the McCracken and Signal mines lured people to the growing town. Within a few months there were two hundred buildings and almost eight hundred inhabitants. Signal's prize feature was a brewery.

In the camp's early years isolation from freighting sources was a major concern. Supplies from San Francisco arrived at Signal via rail to the west side of the Colorado River at Yuma, thence by barge up the river to Aubrey Landing, and finally thirty-five miles by mule team. This slow and laborious method of receiving supplies was somewhat disconcerting to Signal merchants, who had to order their goods six months in advance.

The initial boom and excitement soon passed. By the mid-1880's Signal's population had decreased to about three hundred industrious, law-abiding people. Moses Levy, the justice of the peace, was rarely called upon to exercise his judicial powers. The low rate of misdemeanors and felonies was attributed to Levy's extreme sentences. It was better to obey the law than to incite his anger.

During the ensuing years Signal followed a trend of ups and downs. Eventually mining became too sporadic to support the town.

Liverpool Landing, also called Pittsburgh, was a former steamboat landing on the Colorado River. It probably served as a supply point for the mines at Signal and other camps in the Owens district during the 1880's and 1890's. Little else is known about it.

Signal—the only remaining signs of Signal are this old saloon, a cemetery, and piles of rubble.

Silent and Norton's Landing

SILENT—COUNTY: *Yuma*
LOCATION: *about 21 mi. north of Yuma*
MAP: *page 179*
P.O. est. as Silent, Nov. 8, 1880; discont. March 13, 1884.
NORTON'S LANDING—COUNTY: *Yuma*
LOCATION: *about 20 mi. north of Yuma*
MAP: *page 179*
P.O. est. as Norton's, June 4, 1883; discont. March 13, 1894.

The Silver district renewed activity when George Sills, Neils Johnson, George W. Norton, and Gus Crawford relocated many abandoned claims in 1879. Some of the mines were the Black Rock, Pacific, Red Cloud, Silver Glance, and Princess. A mill was erected near the Red Cloud, around which Silent grew.

Silent was unique. Due to the lack of lumber and a scarcity of water for adobe, inhabitants dug rather than built their homes. Along Black Rock Wash, caves were carved out of the hard mudstone bank. Some of the homes consisted of one large room with a hearth at the far end, while others were merely shallow holes.

Buildings comprised Silent's business district. Three general merchandise stores, a hotel, and a post office were listed in 1882. A combination saloon and dance hall known as "La Cantina La Plata" provided the camp's night life.

Ore from the mines was hauled down a wash to Norton's Landing on the Colorado River, where the Red Cloud Mining Company ran a small smelter. Originally settled in 1870, Norton's lists a population of thirty, a post office, and a general store in the mid 1880's.

Both Silent and Norton's Landing died when silver prices took a tumble in 1893.

Silent. In the early history of Silent, miners lived in dugouts such as this. The opening is about five feet high, with an additional eight feet of boulder-earth bank above.

Ruins of the La Cantina La Plata, a dance hall and saloon, at the Red Cloud Mine, Silent.

Silverbell

COUNTY: *Pima*
LOCATION: *24 mi. west of Marana*
MAP: *page 185*
P.O. est. as Silverbell, Aug. 18, 1904.

Silverbell's prosperity was based on copper. As early as the 1860's, high-grade ore was discovered in the area. Several companies organized, acquired claims, and worked the ore until 1883, when low copper prices discouraged these efforts.

The Mammoth and Old Boot mines at Silverbell were obtained by E. B. Gage and W. F. Staunton in 1902. With the Development Company of America, they organized the Imperial Copper Company. Mining activity began to boom and so did the newly established camp of Silverbell. With the completion of the Arizona Southern Railroad from Red Rock to Silverbell in 1904, the erection of the Sasco smelter, and an acquired population of three thousand, Silverbell veered into prominence as one of the most renowned mining camps in the southwest.

A bad shaft fire at Silverbell in 1911 and water difficulties at their Tombstone properties eventually caused the Development Company of America to go bankrupt, and ended their activity at Silverbell. The American Smelting and Refining Company took over in 1915 and operated until low copper prices halted production in 1921. In 1934 the tracks of the Arizona Southern Railroad to Red Rock were torn up, and the Sasco smelter dismantled. By then, Silverbell's fame had expired.

Once described as: "The hell-hole of Arizona," Silverbell gained notoriety through various reported murders and other lawless acts. Much of Silverbell's roughness was tamed by Deputy Sam McEven. Three days before McEven arrived at Silverbell to execute his new job as deputy, three murders had been committed. McEven spent the first few months on the job disarming, jailing, and fining local desperadoes for carrying concealed weapons.

After Ramon Castro killed Gracio Manzo, he hid from the law for two weeks in an abandoned mine tunnel. As deputy, it was McEven's duty to bring the culprit to justice, yet he knew that if he entered the tunnel without sufficient protection, he would be a perfect target for the killer. He devised a simple but effective shield. Obtaining an ore car, upon which he hung a lamp, McEven pushed the bulletproof barrier ahead of him through the underground tunnels until he had cornered and captured Castro.

The new town of Silver Bell, established in 1948, is located about four miles southeast of the old Silverbell site. The original mining camp has completely vanished. Not a trace remains of its past glory.

Silverbell, circa 1906.—Courtesy University of Arizona, Special Collections

Advertisement, 1905.—*Courtesy Arizona Pioneers' Historical Society*

140
S

One of Silverbell's three cemeteries.

Silverbell, *circa 1910.—Courtesy American Smelting and Refining Co. and Ray Manley*

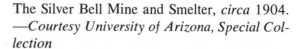

The Silver Bell Mine and Smelter, *circa* 1904. *—Courtesy University of Arizona, Special Collection*

Silverbell, 1932. Two abandoned engines of the Arizona Southern Railroad used from Red Rock Station to Silverbell between 1904 and 1934.—*Courtesy Arizona Pioneers' Historical Society*

Silver King

County: *Pinal*
Location: *about 5 mi. north of Superior*
Map: *page 191*
P.O. est. as Silver King, Dec. 21, 1877; discont. May 5, 1912.

The fabulous Silver King Mine was really discovered twice. In 1873, General George Stoneman, forced to apply more effective measures toward controlling the marauding Apaches, began construction on a road leading from Camp Picketpost, near the present site of Superior, into the Pinal Mountains. This road, allowing greater accessibility to Apache retreats, was known as Stoneman's Grade. A soldier named Sullivan, assigned to the work detail, picked up some black metallic rocks while returning to camp one evening. Although he was not familiar with raw silver, the fact that the rocks flattened when he tried to break them aroused his curiosity, so he kept several. Shortly thereafter, Sullivan's term of service expired and he went to work on Charles Mason's ranch. Frequently Sullivan would show the metallic pieces to Mason and others, but he would never reveal exactly where he had found them. One day Sullivan disappeared, and it was believed that Apaches had killed him. There followed several unsuccessful attempts to locate the source of Sullivan's silver. Then, in 1875, Mason, Benjamin W. Regan, William H. Long, Isaac Copeland, and another companion, went to the Globe mines. On their return trip they were attacked by Apaches and a member of their party was killed. The survivors took the victim's body to Stoneman's former camp and buried it in a stone baking oven. Meanwhile, one of their mules strayed away, and Copeland was sent in pursuit. While securing the animal, which he found at the foot of Stoneman's Grade, Copeland stumbled over a projecting silver outcropping. It proved to be the same outcrop that Sullivan had discovered earlier.

Years later, in 1882 when the mine was producing at full scale and flourishing Silver King community was reaping its profits, a shabbily dressed man appeared at the mine looking for work. He was Sullivan, the original discoverer.

At first the ore from the Silver King Mine was shipped to San Francisco to be smelted. Then a mill was erected at Pinal and twenty-mule teams hauled the ore there to be processed. Concentrates were then freighted on to San Francisco.

Silver King grew rapidly as the price of silver held firm. The town contained two hotels owned respectively by Bob Williams and Bill O'Boyle. Naturally there was some jealousy between the two—both would have preferred a monopoly. The outcome of their petty rivalry was a shooting match. Since both lacked the finesse of gunmen, neither was seriously injured, but for several days Bob Williams was forced to take his meals standing up.

Reverend G. H. Adams approached Perry Wildman, postmaster and owner of a general store, and suggested that Perry find a place where religious services could be held. The task was easy. Wildman simply made the rounds of the saloons, approached each gambling table and told the boys that they needed a church. A hat was passed around and all the men threw in coins. More donations at the mine and elsewhere made a grand total of twelve hundred dollars. The new building, serving a threefold purpose as church, school, and dancehall, was built by volunteer labor on a small rise called the "Hill of Science." Maintenance costs were defrayed by holding dances.

Silver King's death blow came in 1888 with the drop in the price of silver. The King closed and the population of several hundred people dispersed in every direction, leaving their historic camp to die.

One lonely, deserted two-story building stands as the only remaining relic of Silver King. Having once housed the offices of the Silver King Mining Company and the living quarters of the mine superintendent, it is now a tourist curiosity.

Advertisement, 1881.—*Courtesy Arizona Pioneers' Historical Society*

Silver King, 1884. A woodcut of Perry Wildman's General Store, *History of Arizona Territory*. Wallace W. Elliot Publishing Co., San Francisco, 1884.

General George Stoneman (1822–94). Stoneman was a cavalry captain with the Mormon Battalion in 1846. In 1870 he built a fort at Pinal Ranch and commanded the military activities against the Apaches until after the Camp Grant Massacre in 1871, when General Crook relieved him of his duties. Stoneman served as governor of California from 1883 to 1887. — *Courtesy Library of Congress*

Silver King—building that once housed the offices for the Silver
King Mine.

The town of Silver King, *circa* 1880, looking northeast. The building in the right center appears to be the one remaining building shown above.—*Courtesy Arizona Pioneers' Historical Society*

Stanton

COUNTY: *Yavapai*
LOCATION: *8 mi. east of Congress Junction*
MAP: *pages 183-189*
P.O. est. as Stanton, March 5, 1875; discont. June 15, 1905.

History has branded Charles P. Stanton as shrewd, conniving, and avaricious. Perhaps he was. Many brutal deeds he allegedly instigated mark his ruthless and criminal climb to power.

Stanton came to Arizona from Nevada about 1869 and landed a job as assayer at the Vulture mill near Wickenburg. While there, he somehow managed to acquire half-interest in a prospect named the Leviathan, near Rich Hill. After the mill shut down, Stanton went to Antelope Creek near the Leviathan and built a cabin and, eventually, a store. Apparently, as early as 1863 a small nucleus of people had collected in the shadow of Rich Hill, forming a mining community. A stage station, known as Antelope Station, was maintained here by Yaqui Wilson. Another station was set up about half a mile from Wilson's place by an old Englishman named Partridge. Stanton, envious of the two men, began to plot a diabolical scheme. If he could do away with both men he could have the road run by his own place and capture all the business build up by Wilson and Partridge. Since Wilson and Partridge were competitors, it was easy for Stanton to work the men into a feud over their opposing businesses. Partridge eventually became sufficiently riled so that he killed Wilson. Tried and found guilty of murder, Partridge was sent to Yuma Territorial Prison, where he claimed that the ghost of Wilson haunted him every night in his cell. However, Stanton's plot fell short of its goal. Wilson had a silent partner named Timmerman who took over the station, and creditors promptly sold Partridge's place to Barney Martin.

Meanwhile, Stanton had befriended Francisco Vega, a cold-blooded murderer who led a gang of homicidal desperados. Now Stanton could simply hire Vega to carry out any criminal deed he wanted committed. After disposing of Timmerman, his next victim was Barney Martin. In addition to the station, Martin owned a small cattle ranch. In July of 1886 he sold his ranch. With the money, Martin promised his wife and sons a trip east while he enlarged his station. On July 21 the Martin family loaded up their wagon for the two-day trip to Phoenix whence Mrs. Martin and the children would depart for the east. They never reached Phoenix. Some weeks later, their charred bodies and burnt wagon were found a few miles from Antelope Station, by this time known as Stanton. There was not enough definite proof to convict anyone, but rumor linked certain names to the murders.

A few months later, on November 13, Stanton was seated at a table in his store, reading. Two Mexican toughs entered and opened fire, killing him. Cristo Lucero, a former member of the Vega gang, was revenging an insult Stanton had made to his sister.

The community, composed of about two hundred miners, their scattered tents and shacks, and Stanton's store, expanded by the 1890's to envelop a five-stamp mill, boardinghouse, a dozen or more houses, and a new store. Several buildings still occupy the townsite.

Stanton—at the base of Rich Hill, looking north.

Old hotel in present-day Stanton.

Stanton before 1886—Stanton Store and famous Charles Stanton.—*Courtesy Sharlot Hall Museum*

Stockton

COUNTY: *Mohave*
LOCATION: *about 8 mi. north of Kingman*
MAP: *page 175*
P.O. est. as Stockton, March 7, 1888; discont. July 11, 1892.

Principal mines at Stockton Hill were discovered in the early 1860's. Twenty years later a small but prosperous community had grown to meet the needs of the miners. By 1884 the rich silver-bearing mines boosted Stockton into first place as the liveliest mining camp in Mohave County. Mills at Mineral Park and Cerbat treated the ore before it was shipped to smelters in San Francisco and New Mexico.

A few deserted buildings, possibly of a later date, still nestle at the base of Stockton Hill.

Stoddard

Stoddard, *circa* 1885—tent buildings.
—*Courtesy Sharlot Hall Museum*

COUNTY: *Yavapai*
LOCATION: *about 5 mi. east of Mayer*
MAP: *page 189*
P.O. est. as Stoddard, Dec. 15, 1882; discont.
   Sept. 15, 1927.

A camp named in honor of Isaac T. Stoddard, an important figure in the exploitation of northern Arizona's mineral wealth, served the Stoddard and Binghampton copper mines. Founded about 1880 on the Agua Fria River, Stoddard contained the first copper-smelting plant put into operation in that district.

As late as 1925, Stoddard reported a hundred residents, a school, boardinghouse, and general merchandise store. Shortly afterward, the postwar slump in copper prices brought an end to the camp's activities.

Birdsells Boarding House in Stoddard, *circa* 1900.—*Courtesy Sharlot Hall Museum*

Stoddard, *circa* 1900—looking north along the Agua Fria River.—*Courtesy University of Arizona, Special Collections*

Sunnyside

COUNTY: *Cochise*

LOCATION: *about 15 mi. southwest of Fort Huachuca*

MAP: *page 195*

P.O. est. as Sunnyside, July 16, 1914; discont. March 15, 1934.

Situated high in the Huachuca Mountains, the Copper Glance Mine once supported what was probably Arizona's most unusual mining camp. Here lived a community devoted to hymn singing, Bible reading, and brotherly love instead of the typical hard drinking, gambling, and coarse language prevalent in most mining towns. Sunnyside was a small religious colony founded by Samuel Donnelly.

Some rumors claim that Donnelly was a patron of the waterfront bars in San Francisco before receiving his calling. Whether this is true or not is questionable. Nonetheless, Donnelly acquired religion, went to Tombstone, relocated the Copper Glance Mine in 1887, and became preacher and leader of a cult known as the Donnellites. Donnelly was not affiliated with any denomination nor did he advocate any new theological dogmas. The word of the Bible provided his inspiration and guide.

The Donnellites lived as one large family. The men worked the mine and then pooled all the money to be used for the entire community. Although each family had their separate cabin, everyone ate in a community kitchen run by the women of the camp. Provisions and supplies for Sunnyside were packed over the mountains from Tombstone or Fairbank. Each person contributed his or her special talents or skills toward the betterment of the camp. The woman best qualified for teaching taught Sunnyside's twenty-four pupils, Lillian Crawford gave piano lessons, and Mr. Cushing gave violin lessons. When the day's work was over, all would congregate to sing hymns or listen to "Brother" Donnelly speak.

It would be easy enough for an isolated religious colony such as Sunnyside to be divorced from the needs of the outside world. Not so with Donnelly's camp. He preached charity, and they all practiced it. Once Mr. Donnelly visited the University of Arizona at Tucson and found some Cochise County students in need of financial assistance. These students, working their way through college, earning $8.50 a month were faced with monthly expenses of $13. Donnelly generously donated an allowance of $20 a month to each student. Once a prospector stopped at Sunnyside and asked to buy some provisions. The Donnellites amply supplied him with beef, beans, and tobacco. They would take nothing in return, telling the prospector that their only desire was to do good to their fellow men.

After Donnelly died, the Donnellites held together for several years, until the mine closed. Then the colony disbanded because the men had to get out to make a living.

The Donnellites are gone, but a few of their deserted wooden homes and their schoolhouse still stand in the quiet serenity of a small mountain meadow.

Sunnyside, 1963. Left, E. R. Langford house; right rear, schoolhouse.—*Courtesy Historical Museum, Fort Hauchuca*

Swansea

COUNTY: *Yuma*
LOCATION: *about 30 mi. east of Parker*
MAP: *page 177*
P.O. est. as Swansea, March 25, 1909; discont. June 28, 1924.

Swansea flourished for a number of years as the headquarters for the Clara Consolidated Gold and Copper Mining Company. A branch railroad built from Swansea to connect with the Santa Fe at Bouse in 1908 soon provided the camp with a reported 200 to 300 inhabitants. The population eventually grew to 750.

Originally known as Signal, Swansea adopted its present name with the establishment of a post office in 1909. The camp was provided with an electric light company, an automobile dealer, a lumber and realty company, general merchandise stores, saloons, restaurants, a barber, physician, justice of the peace, notary public, and insurance agent.

By 1912, Clara Consolidated Gold and Copper Mining Company had collapsed into bankruptcy, but various other companies kept the town active until the mine closed in 1924.

Swansea—ruins of Main Street.

One of the two cemeteries at Swansea, looking north toward the Bill Williams River.

Swansea, *circa* 1910. The beginning of a copper camp.—*Courtesy Sharlot Hall Museum*

Tiger

COUNTY: *Pinal*
LOCATION: *4 mi. west of Mammoth*
MAP: *page 193*
P.O. est. as Schultz, July 12, 1894; discont. May 15, 1902. P.O. est. as Tiger, March 15, 1939; discont. Nov. 26, 1954.

In 1881, Frank Schultz located the ore body that developed into the Mammoth Mine. The ensuing camp adopted the name Schultz. Lack of water at the mine prompted erection of a mill on the banks of the San Pedro at the present town of Mammoth. At first the ore was hauled from the mine to the mill, a distance of three miles, by mule teams and wagons. By 1903 an aerial tramway had been constructed to transport the ore.

Schultz renewed activity as Tiger after Sam Houghton purchased the mine property following World War I. He renamed both the town and the mine for the mascot of his alma mater, Princeton University. Tiger achieved a peak population of about eighteen hundred residents.

Nothing is left of Tiger today, since the San Manuel Copper Company razed the camp buildings.

Schultz, 1903.—Courtesy Arizona Pioneers' Historical Society

Mammoth, 1895. Interior of the stamp mill where gold ore from the Mammoth Mine was processed. —*Courtesy University of Arizona, Special Collections*

Mammoth, 1896. This smelter at Mammoth reduced the ore from the mines at Schultz.—*Courtesy University of Arizona, Special Collections*

Tip Top

COUNTY: *Yavapai*
LOCATION: *about 45 mi. northwest of Phoenix*
MAP: *page 189*
P.O. est. as Tip Top, Aug. 12, 1880; discont. Feb. 14, 1895.

Two men named Moore and Corning located the Tip Top silver mine in 1875. A year later miners had settled Tip Top camp. Before long there were over two hundred inhabitants, including about fifteen youngsters and eight women. Despite its size, Tip Top lacked a post office for several years. The camp people had to pay $30 a month to have their mail delivered from the mill town of Gillett, eight miles away. By 1880, Tip Top had acquired the much-needed post office.

Although many of Tip Top's miners were veterans of the Civil War, both Union and Confederate, they were essentially compatible. Firearms were worn and used, not for claim jumpers or bar-

room brawls, but for renegade Indians. A few killings were scattered throughout Tip Top's history. Two men were killed in gun fights, one by lightning, and a fourth by a centipede bite. The latter episode occurred when a miner, on rising in the morning, pulled on his boot and was bitten on the toe by the varmint. Since liquor was considered a panacea, the frightened miner rushed to the nearest saloon and gulped down a quart of whisky. Needless to say, he died. There was some question as to whether his death was caused by the poison or the antidote.

Once a preacher from Phoenix came to the camp to save a few souls. There being no church, he held services outside under some cottonwood trees. All the miners came to hear him. Sitting under the trees drinking their beer, they thoroughly enjoyed the sermon. Afterward the miners generously donated to the preacher's cause.

Tip Top was well supplied, with a grade school, two general stores, six saloons, two restaurants, a Chinese laundry, feed yard, blacksmith shop, butcher shop, and shoe store.

The drop in the price of silver forced Tip Top out of existence. By 1895 it was a dead camp, but its ruins still straggle along the canyon.

View of the south end of Tip Top, *circa* 1888. (1) stamp mill, (2) mine office.—*Courtesy Sharlot Hall Museum*

View of the north end of Tip Top, *circa* 1888. (1) stamp mill, (2) assay office, (3) brewery, (4) beer hall, (5) restaurant, (6) saloon, (7) hotel, (8) mine workings.—*Courtesy Sharlot Hall Museum*

Tombstone

COUNTY: *Cochise*
LOCATION: *24 mi. southeast of Benson*
MAP: *page 195*
P.O. est. as Tombstone, Dec. 2, 1878.

Tailed by a colorful and romantic history, Tombstone is, without doubt, the most famous of Arizona's mining camps.

Ed Schieffelin, son of one of the forty-niners, came to Arizona in 1877. At that time Apaches were on the warpath, preventing prospectors from developing the mineral deposits known to exist in the San Pedro region. Ed Schieffelin, however, could not be dissuaded by the thought of death at the hands of the Apaches. After traveling with the cavalry from San Bernardino, California, to Fort Huachuca, Schieffelin announced his intentions of exploring the San Pedro Valley. His soldier companions warned him that he would find only his tombstone in the Apaches' domain, but the persistent prospector, undaunted by the ominous prognosis, set out alone, late in 1877. In February of 1878 his energy and courage were rewarded. Schieffelin found a silver float, traced it to a rich ledge, and staked the Tombstone and Graveyard claims.

Since there was no assay office at that time in Tucson, Ed took some of the samples north to the Signal Mine, where his brother Al was working. The company assayer at the Signal, Richard K. Gird, immediately recognized the samples as high-grade ore. After persuading the brothers to accept him as a partner, Richard Gird departed for the San Pedro Valley with Ed and Al Schieffelin.

When the Graveyard claim proved to be only a disappointing pocket, Ed continued prospecting. In two successive days he discovered the Lucky Cuss and Toughnut deposits. Shortly afterward the Contention and Grand Central deposits were staked. From these four mines, millions of dollars worth of silver were taken between 1880 and 1886.

The original camp which followed the fabulous strikes had a different name and location from present-day Tombstone. Established in the vicinity of the Lucky Cuss Mine, a settlement known as Watervale became the center of activity until mid-1879. Then the location of the town moved to a mesa overlooking the Toughnut Mine and here, in April, 1879, the first house in Tombstone was erected.

The small hamlet quickly stretched out in every direction, discarding its temporary canvas tents and shanties for permanent buildings. By 1880, Tombstone had boomed into the most famous mining camp in the west. In that year telegraph connections were installed, gas soon replaced oil for lighting, and houses grew by the score. Tombstone was incorporated as a city in 1881. In addition to the usual number of general and special stores there were Catholic, Presbyterian, Episcopal, and Methodist churches, a good school employing five teachers and attended by 250 pupils, an iron foundry, a bottling works, a city hall, two banks, and a newspaper, the *Epitaph*. In 1882 Tombstone reputedly had 150 licensed establishments dispensing liquor.

Twice Tombstone had near deathblows. Once in June, 1881, and again in May, 1882, fires swept through the town, leaving charred ruins. Both times Tombstone was rebuilt, bigger and better, to meet the needs of the expanding population, which eventually reached a peak of fifteen thousand.

Many acts of lawlessness contributed to Tombstone's notoriety throughout the west. Possibly no other story is as well known as the famous gun fight at OK Corral. The fight, climaxing a long-standing feud between the Earp and Clanton factions, erupted into a deadly gun battle on October 26, 1881. City Marshal Virgil Earp, aided by his two brothers, Wyatt and Morgan, and Doc Holliday, attempted to disarm Ike and Billy Clanton and the McLowery brothers, who were openly making threats on his life. In the few seconds that guns were fired, Tom and Frank McLowery fell dead and Billy Clanton, seriously wounded, died half an hour later.

Tombstone continued to be a rough, tough, hell-raising town until the five-man hanging in March, 1884. After this episode, peace became more popular than outlawry. On December 6, 1883, five armed men strode into Goldwater & Castenada General Store in Bisbee, robbed the place, and left four dead victims. A sheriff's posse eventually caught up with the outlaws and landed the five in the county jail at Tombstone. A sixth member of the gang was apprehended shortly afterward, and paid for his part two weeks earlier than the others. It appeared that John Heath, a saloonkeeper, was one of the first Bisbee citizens to help form a posse to ride after the murderers. His anxiety to lead the posse away from the obvious trail quickly caused suspicion to center on him. Heath was arrested, given a separate trial, found guilty of being an accessory to the crime, and sentenced to life imprisonment. Angry Bisbee and Tombstone citizens felt that Heath deserved death. On February 22, 1884, a raging mob of miners stormed the Tombstone jail, dragged Heath to a telephone pole, and lynched him.

The execution date for the five other prisoners was set for March 8, 1884. Official invitations to the hanging were issued. Some sadistic citizens built a tier of seats around the scaffold and were going to charge fifty cents for admission. Fortunately, a sympathetic group demolished the bleachers the night before the execution. The hanging took place as scheduled, and Omar W. Sample, James Howard, Daniel Dowd, W. E. Delaney, and Daniel Kelly paid for their crimes.

When fire destroyed the pumping works at the Grand Central Mine in 1886, water flooded the mines and operations were suspended. Tombstone's lusty years were ended.

Today, thousands of tourists visit Tombstone annually, viewing the many historical landmarks still intact. Boot Hill Cemetery, decked with amusing epitaphs; the Bird Cage Theater, built as a combination theater and dance hall saloon in 1881; St. Paul's Episcopal Church, the oldest Protestant church still standing in Arizona; and the stately adobe Schieffelin Hall, built as a civic and social center, are a few of the major attractions.

Tombstone, 1881—looking north from the Toughnut Mine.— *Courtesy Arizona Pioneers' Historical Society*

Edward Schieffelin (1847–97).—*Courtesy John Gilchriese*

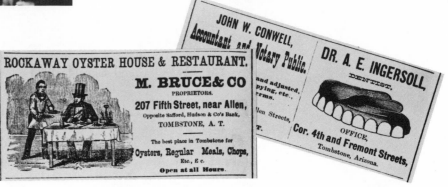

Above—Tombstone, 1884. John Heath was lynched February 22, 1884, for his part in a robbery and killings that occurred in Bisbee.—*Courtesy Arizona Pioneers' Historical Society*

Right — Advertisements. — *Courtesy Arizona Pioneers' Historical Society*

Tombstone, 1882 — Fremont Street after the fire in May of 1882.—*Courtesy Arizona Pioneers' Historical Society*

Virgil Earp (1843–1906), city marshall of Tombstone.—*Courtesy Arizona Pioneers' Historical Society*

Wyatt Earp (1848–1929), photograph taken in 1926.—*Courtesy Arizona Pioneers' Historical Society*

Tombstone, 1963. (1) Schieffelin Hall, (2) OK Corral street fight, (3) shooting of Virgil Earp, December, 1881, (4) Old Epitaph office, (5) Courtroom where Doc Holliday and Wyatt Earp were tried for the OK Corral street fight, (6) Nellie Cashman's Russ House, (7) Old Cochise County Courthouse.—*Courtesy Arizona Pioneers' Historical Society*

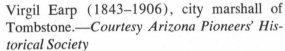

Total Wreck

COUNTY: *Pima*
LOCATION: *9 mi. south of Pantano*
MAP: *page 195*
P.O. est. as Total Wreck, Aug. 12, 1881; discont. Nov. 1, 1890.

John L. Dillon discovered a silver-lead mine in the Empire Mountains in 1879. When asked what he was going to name the claim he replied that he did not know, but that the hill on which the ledge was located looked like a total wreck. The name stuck.

Little was done at the mine until the coming of the railroad in 1881. That year the Empire Mining and Developing Company purchased the property and installed a seventy-ton mill.

Total Wreck camp followed in close pursuit of the mining activity. By 1883 there were two hundred inhabitants, fifty houses, three stores, three hotels, four saloons, a butcher shop and a lumber yard.

One June day in 1883 a number of Mexicans hired to cut wood to be used as fuel for the mill were occupied at their task on the west side of the Whetstone Mountains. Some of Geronimo's Apaches made a surprise attack, killing six of the woodcutters and driving off a team of their mules. These were the first victims to be buried in Total Wreck's small cemetery.

A rather bizarre shooting occurred at Total Wreck. Mr. E. B. Salsig got into a dispute with another man, who drew his gun and fired. Salsig would have been killed except for the fact that he had a large package of love-letters stuffed in his vest pocket. The bullet lodged in the letters, thus preventing his death. Later he married the lady who had written the letters.

By the end of 1884 the mine and mill were closed. Later the property was sold for taxes.

Above—Total Wreck, present ruins.

Left — Total Wreck, *circa* 1885. (1) dining room and office, (2) assay office, (3) miners lodging house, (4) lodging house, (5) saloon, (6) butcher shop, (7) Edward L. Vail residence. — *Courtesy Arizona Pioneers' Historical Society*

Troy, *circa* 1900 — looking north. — *Courtesy Charles Bronson*

Troy—present-day site viewed from the same angle as the above picture.

Troy

COUNTY: *Pinal*
LOCATION: *about 14 mi. southeast of Superior*
MAP: *page 191*
P.O. est. as Troy, Aug. 5, 1901; discont. Sept. 15, 1910.

By 1903 two companies had consolidated to form the Troy Manhattan Copper Company and were developing the mines at Troy, originally known as Skinnerville.

Early citizens of the camp took advantage of an Arizona option law to exclude saloons and to adopt prohibition within the confines of the community. As a result of this action, Troy became known as a model mining camp.

In 1903 an array of tents accommodated the residents of the camp, and seven wooden-frame company buildings housed the general store, hospital, boardinghouse, assaying laboratories, and assorted offices. There were also a schoolhouse and a combination union hall and reading room. The latter, built by the Troy Miners' Union, was well stocked with magazines, periodicals and news-papers. Here the miners and their families spent many leisure hours. Troy boasted a municipal water system and a splendid brass band. The population numbered about two hundred people.

Copper ore from the mines was transported to Kelvin by the narrowest narrow-gauge railroad in the territory. The biggest feature of the engine was the smoke stack.

Private ranch buildings now occupy the site.

Twin Buttes, *circa* 1905. Miners waiting to be transferred underground.—*Arizona Pioneers' Historical Society*

Twin Buttes

COUNTY: *Pima*
LOCATION: *20 mi. south of Tucson*
MAP: *page 195*
P.O. est. as Twin Buttes, Dec. 29, 1906; discont. Aug. 15, 1930.

The discovery of copper in the Twin Buttes region is accredited to three prospectors known as "The Three Nations"—John G. Baxter, American (Wisconsin), Michael Irish, of Ireland, and John Ellis, of Scotland. After struggling for years to develop a few small prospects, they interested Mayor David S. Rose of Milwaukee and a number of prominent investors in taking over the property. In 1903 Twin Buttes Mining and Smelting Company developed and operated the Senator, Morgan, Copper Glance, Copper Queen, and Copper King mines. The company shipped ore to the smelters at Sasco and elsewhere until 1914.

Meanwhile, Twin Buttes camp had sprung to life. A bunkhouse, assay office, store, boarding-house, and school were built. Establishment of a post office and completion of the railroad branch connecting the growing metropolis with the Southern Pacific Tucson-Nogales line at Sahuarita were milestones of 1906. The formal railroad dedication, held on July 4 of that year, took place at the new Twin Buttes Railroad Station.

After a series of ups and downs, Twin Buttes, unable to support its three hundred residents, became a ghost town.

The few buildings left standing are posted against trespassers.

THE TWIN BUTTES TIMES

VOL. I.   TWIN BUTTES CAMP, ARIZONA, FEBRUARY, 1905.   No. 1.

THE TWIN BUTTES

This camp takes its name from two sister "buttes" rising abruptly from the mesa, in whose shadows the camp rests. It is one of the most picturesquely delightful locations in the whole territory. To the north may be seen the Tucson mountains whose jagged crags mark the horizon line. To the right of them but a third of a century he has followed the calling of a miner. Educated beyond the average of his fellows his many years with the "bit and hammer" have brought to him rich knowledge of a practical kind and made his judgment valuable to all who may become possessed of it.

John Ellis is a native born Scotchman. Rugged, persevering, industrious, he has had broad experience in many of the great camps of the west and southwest.

ELLIS.   BAXTER.   IRISH.

THE NEW COMERS

DAVID S ROSE.

DR. WM. H. EARLES.

Dr. William H. Earles, the treasurer of the company, is and for years has been a successful medical practitioner at the city of Milwaukee.

HON. HUGH RYAN.

Hon. Hugh Ryan, one of Wisconsin's leading lawyers, is likewise a director and takes an active interest in the company's affairs.

PHIL C. BRANNEN.

Mr. Phil C. Brannen, another director, is one of the successful business men of Tucson.

H. J. BLAKELEY.

Mr. H. J. Blakely, who now resides at Tucson, is step-son to Mayor Rose, and is secretary of the company.

DR. FRED R. WEBER.

Dr. Fred R. Weber, of Milwaukee, visited the mines about the time that the last annual meeting was held.

ENGINE HOUSE IN THE MORGAN.

TWIN BUTTES RAILROAD COMPANY.

The question of transportation is always an important factor in the consideration of mining operations.

GRADING THE RAILROAD.

GRADING CAMP.

Concluded on page 2.

161
T

Twin Buttes, 1905. Front page of the first Twin Buttes newspaper.—*Courtesy Arizona Pioneers' Historical Society*

Vekol—adobe ruins.

Vekol

COUNTY: *Pinal*

LOCATION: *about 30 mi. southwest of Casa Grande*

MAP: *page 185*

P.O. est. as Vekol, Sept. 25, 1888; discont. Oct. 30, 1909.

John D. Walker, P. R. Brady, and Juan Jose Gradello located the Vekol silver mine on February 5, 1880. Soon afterward, Gradello dropped out of the picture, and Walker's brother Lucien took over a third interest.

Vekol camp was equipped with a store, boardinghouse, post office, school, public library and reading room, and comfortable homes. Because of some carousing, the mining company forbade their employees to patronize the local saloon. Consequently, Vekol's one saloon went out of business, and the camp became quiet and orderly. There was no jail and apparently no need for one. If an employee committed a misdemeanor, he was automatically discharged from his job and escorted from camp.

Since the discovery of the mine, John Walker had been recognized as head of the mining company. Lucien envied his brother. After John had a slight stroke, Lucien and a third brother, William, seized upon the opportunity to have him committed to an insane asylum. It was easy for them to do this, since John, by nature, was eccentric. Next, they appointed themselves official guardians of their brother's wealth. After a short stay in the

asylum, John was released. He went to Tucson and got married in April of 1891 to Ellinor Rice, his sweetheart for many years. Realizing that John's fortune would now lawfully go to the new Mrs. Walker, the brothers tried by every legal means to have John and his wife separated. No doubt it was the covetous demands of his brothers that actually drove John to the breaking point. On September 2, 1891, he died in Napa Insane Asylum.

After John Walker's death, the legal battle began between his widow and his brothers over who should inherit the mine and property worth about $3,000,000. About this time, another claimant to the fortune appeared on the scene—Juana Walker, half-blood daughter of John and an Indian squaw named Juanita. Lucien and William tried to prove that John had never been married to Juana's mother, but they failed. Records showed that Walker and the Indian woman had been married in accordance with the tribal rites and legally had been man and wife.

The Walker case dragged on for many years, progressing from the Probate Court of Pinal County to the United States Supreme Court. There a verdict was reached in 1907 in favor of Lucien and William. Juana's claim to her father's wealth was rejected on the grounds that marriage between an Indian and a white was not valid.

During the decade of the 1880's, Vekol was an active silver producing camp. Following John Walker's death, the camp slid into a period of inactivity. A change of hands and new interest rejuvenated Vekol during the early years of the twentieth century. The camp embraced about 165 people, including several families.

Remnants of four adobe buildings, rock foundations, and mill ruins remain.

Vekol—looking northwest over the townsite.

Venezia

COUNTY: *Yavapai*
LOCATION: *about 20 mi. south of Prescott*
MAP: *page 189*
P.O. est. as Venezia, April 16, 1916; discont. June 1, 1935.

As early as 1880 mining activity was taking place on the south side of Mt. Union some twenty miles south of Prescott. In 1916 the Venezia post office was established in that locality. F. Scopel, local settler and Italian immigrant, named the camp for his native city, Venice. By 1925 Venezia's inhabitants numbered seventy-three. Mining and stock-raising were the principal industries. The village businesses included a general merchandise store and a stage line to Crown King.

Today, collapsed buildings mark the site.

Venezia—present-day ruins. The mines around Venezia produced close to $750,000 in gold during the early 1900's.

Virginia City

COUNTY: *Mohave*
LOCATION: *about 22 mi. south of Wikieup*
MAP: *page 177*
P.O. none.

Situated directly across the arroyo from the town of Signal was Virginia City or New Virginia. Actually, the line of demarcation between Signal and Virginia was so nebulous that the two could well have been considered one town. Yet they were not. Each boasted its own individual appeal. Signal had the post office, but Virginia City claimed the twenty-stamp McCracken mill which sustained both communities.

In addition to a foundry, machine-shop, smelting and refining works, and company offices clustered by the mill, Virginia City also had a good drugstore, first-rate hotel and saloon, restaurant, general store, and a few scattered dwellings. The population ranged between six and seven hundred in 1877.

Ruins of the McCracken mill are still visible.

Vulture City

COUNTY: *Maricopa*
LOCATION: *13 mi. southwest of Wickenburg*
MAP: *page 183*
P.O. est. as Vulture, Oct. 4, 1880; discont. April 24, 1897.

Henry Wickenburg discovered the rich Vulture gold mine in 1863. Born Heinrich Heintzel in Austria in 1820, Wickenburg came to America and followed the gold furor to the Colorado River. He engaged in prospecting, joined the Weaver party who discovered Rich Hill, and later left the party to look for a mine in the Harqua Hala Mountains. Wickenburg never reached his destination. On the way he came upon an immense quartz projection rich in gold. After doing some mining, Wickenburg began to sell the ore still in the mine at $15 a ton. A purchaser would have to mine, transport, and mill the ore he had bought.

The mine was being worked rather haphazardly until Benjamin Phelps, of Philadelphia, came along. In 1866 he bought four-fifths interest in the Vulture, organized the Vulture Company and erected a twenty-stamp mill on the Hassayampa River.

Eventually, a community grew at the millsite known as Vulture City. There were forty-six dwellings and nearly two hundred inhabitants in 1870.

After all the cottonwood trees and mesquite had been cut to feed the mill, it was moved down the Hassayampa to Seymour. In 1879 the newly-formed Central Arizona Mining Company built twelve miles of six-inch pipeline and erected an eighty-stamp mill at the mine. Soon Vulture City shifted from the Hassayampa to the new milling operation at the Vulture. The town grew to support three hundred residents in the mid-1880's.

By eliminating the expense of hauling the ore and increasing the mill capacity, it was made profitable to process the lower-grade ore. In the early years much of the ore had been tossed aside to be used in constructing buildings at the mine. These buildings were torn down and run through the mill. About two thousand dollars in gold was obtained from the small assay office.

Although Vulture City grew rich and lusty, it was reportedly an extremely dull camp. Stage robberies provided some entertainment. Two strangers named Munroe and Dennis met in Prescott one day in 1881, and formed an alliance to rob the Vulture stage. Their plans made, they started out for Vulture, but not together. Before leaving Prescott, Dennis informed the authorities of his partnership with Munroe, his avowed object being to assist in capturing the potential outlaw. On the day of the planned stage holdup, Munroe observed some Prescott officials hovering around Vulture and at once realized that his partner in crime had sold him out. Searching out Dennis, Munroe accused him of treachery. Dennis denied the charge, then drew his pistol and shot Munroe through the arm. After the doctor had dressed Munroe's fractured arm, the victim of misplaced confidence was placed under the watchful eye of Deputy Sheriff Rogers, outside Charley Genung's meat market. All was quiet until Dennis sauntered into view. The sight of him so enraged Munroe that, despite his injured arm, he knocked Dennis to the ground and proceeded to kick him and pound his head with the butt of his knife until forced away by Charley Genung and the sheriff. A short while later, Munroe, under arrest for assault, was riding as a prisoner in the same coach he had planned to plunder.

In spite of the fact that his mine produced millions of dollars worth of gold, Henry Wickenburg died a pauper. He was shortchanged by Benjamin Phelps, who never paid him the entire amount upon which they had agreed. In his old age, despondent and penniless, Wickenburg ended his own life with a Colt revolver.

Much of the town and the mill have survived the onslaught of time.

Henry Wickenburg (1820–1905). Born in Austria, Wickenburg came to Fort Yuma in 1862. In 1863 he discovered the gold deposit that became the Vulture Mine. A camp established thirteen miles from Vulture grew into the town of Wickenburg.—*Courtesy Arizona Pioneers' Historical Society*

Walker

COUNTY: *Yavapai*
LOCATION: *10 mi. southwest of Prescott*
MAP: *page 189*
P.O. est. as Walker, Dec. 15, 1879; discont. Sept. 30, 1940.

Summer cottages now dot the site of the once bustling gold camp. In the spring of 1863, Captain Joseph Reddeford Walker guided a group of intrepid gold seekers into the heart of central Arizona. The trek was unbelievably difficult. Harassment by Indians and almost insufferable heat added greatly to their hardships. Nevertheless, the courageous Captain Walker, at that time sixty-five years old, managed to lead the expedition from New Mexico to Tucson, west to the Pima villages, across the Gila River, and north along the Hassayampa River.

When the party reached the area around what is now Prescott, they set up a permanent base of operations. The twenty-six men of the original party of thirty-three members felled trees and built a sturdy corral and a fort. Then they branched out, prospecting in all directions. During one excursion, gold was discovered on Lynx Creek. The camp immediately shifted to the newly found gold site. A few log cabins were tossed together and Walker was born.

Mining sustained Walker for some eighty years. The population fluctuated with the times, while new businesses sprang up to replace the ones that closed. As mining waned, the school, jail, hotel, hospital, saloons, pool halls and stores ceased to function as the reported 2,700 residents moved away.

Placer prospector, *circa* 1880's.—*Courtesy Arizona Pioneers' Historical Society*

Washington Camp and Duquesne

COUNTY: *Santa Cruz*
LOCATION: *about 17 mi. east of Nogales*
MAP: *page 195*
P.O. est. as Washington, May 13, 1880; changed to Duquesne, June 6, 1890; discont. Feb. 14, 1920.

Walker, *circa* 1888. Hydraulic Mining on Lynx Creek.—*Courtesy Sharlot Hall Museum*

Ruins of Washington Camp—Duquesne school.

These two camps, so closely allied in location, history, and common interest, can hardly be treated separately.

Prospects were discovered in the area in the early 1860's, but recurrent Apache attacks prevented the region from developing immediately. Although Washington Camp, the older of the two communities, had been settled by the 1870's, it did not begin to prosper until almost 1890, when the Duquesne Mining and Reduction Company of Pittsburgh acquired mining property and founded the town of Duquesne. The company headquarters were established at Duquesne and the reduction plant one mile north at Washington Camp. An immediate spurt of growth took place. A fine new office building, bunkhouses, a boardinghouse, store, butcher shop, and a number of dwellings were built by the company at Washington Camp. Likewise, Duquesne began to mushroom. About 1900, both towns reached their peak populations of approximately a thousand residents.

There is some doubt as to whether the following is true; nevertheless, the story persists that George Westinghouse, of the Westinghouse Electric Company, once resided in Duquesne. Apparently he created quite a stir when he installed luxurious bathrooms with hot and cold running water in his Duquesne home.

A few people still live in both camps. The ruins of the schoolhouse, once attended by children from Washington Camp and Duquesne, is located midway between.

Washington Camp, 1909. Washington Camp and Duquesne Reduction Plant on Washington Gulch, looking west.—*Courtesy U.S. Geological Survey*

Weaver

COUNTY: *Yavapai*

LOCATION: *about 10 mi. east of Congress Junction*

MAP: *pages 183-189*

P.O. est. as Weaver, May 26, 1899; changed to Octave, April 19, 1900.

Certain Indians coming to trade at La Paz in the early 1860's circulated reports of abundant gold deposits to the east. Lured by these rumors, Abraham Harlow Peeples organized a gold-seeking expedition to explore central Arizona. He chose rugged pioneer explorer Pauline Weaver as guide. Their journey eventually led them to the base of Rich Hill. During the night, one of their pack animals strayed up the steep slopes of the table mountain. A Mexican sent to retrieve the beast discovered loose gold nuggets on the mesa top. Rich Hill became the richest placer discovery ever made in Arizona. This discovery also led to the finding of the placers on Weaver and Antelope creeks.

Overnight the area became the scene of intense mining activity as swarms of miners rushed to the bonanza site. A tent city, named in honor of Pauline Weaver, cropped up at the base of Rich Hill, and then gradually gave way to permanent rock and wood buildings.

The early years of Weaver were plagued with some Indian trouble. Sometimes the Indians enjoyed a joke. In December of 1863 there was no grass near Weaver, so the Mexicans who made a living cutting grama grass had to go three or four miles from the camp. They would load their burros with the grama and return to town before nightfall. One particular day about four o'clock, three Mexicans wandered into Weaver stark naked. While they had been at their work, they were startled to find themselves surrounded by Indians. Since the Mexicans were at a disadvantage, they unhesitatingly relinquished their firearms to the redskins. Then the Indians demanded that the Mexicans strip off all their garb. They had no choice; they did as they were told. Departing in triumph, the Indians left the bewildered Mexicans minus guns, burros, and clothes.

As Weaver grew in size and prosperity, so did its unsavory reputation. It became a hangout for thieves and cutthroats. The last bit of lawlessness occurred about 1898—the criminal murder of William Segna, owner of a saloon and mercantile establishment in Weaver. After this, the frightened law-abiding citizens quickly began to move away from Weaver. It was too tough and wicked a place to live. Also, the gold was exhausted. By 1899 the remainder of Weaver had been absorbed into the adjacent mining camp of Octave.

A few prospectors still live at Weaver. There is a small cemetery, and assorted ruins dot the area.

Weaver—cemetery and rock house on the east side of Rich Hill.

Weaver, 1888—Rich Hill in the background.
—*Courtesy Sharlot Hall Museum*

White Hills

COUNTY: *Mohave*
LOCATION: *about 48 mi. northwest of Kingman*
MAP: *page 175*
P.O. est. as White Hills, Oct. 20, 1892; discont. Aug. 15, 1914.

In 1891 an Indian named Hualapai Jeff showed Judge Henry Shaffer a fine specimen of silver he had found when searching for iron oxide to be used as face paint. Shaffer, who at that time was mining at Gold Basin, sought two of his friends, John Burnett and John Sullivan. The three of them, guided by Jeff, traveled to the discovery site, where they located several claims.

News of the find quickly reached the ears of eager prospectors and promoters. A Denver syndicate snatched up the principal claims and installed mining equipment and a mill. The stampede was on to White Hills.

By July 16, 1892, the town—only two weeks old—contained two hundred souls, one store, four saloons, three restaurants, and a string of tents. Residents claimed their town lots by sleeping on their property. After a pleasant night's occupancy on his lot, one particular owner folded up his bedding and found a lively rattlesnake beneath his pillow. Needless to say, the reptile's presence somewhat reduced the man's evaluation of his property.

When an English firm purchased the White Hills claims in 1895, they equipped the town with electric lights, telephones, and running water. White Hills soon became the largest mining camp in Mohave County.

The rich silver could not last forever. As the ore waned, so did the population. Now there are only three dilapidated buildings and no residents in White Hills.

White Hills, *circa* 1905. The mines produced about $2,000,000 worth of gold and silver between 1892 and 1906.—*Courtesy Arizona Pioneers' Historical Society*

White Hills, 1895. Schoolhouse and the class of 1895–96.—*Courtesy Mohave Pioneers' Historical Society*

Abandoned dwellings of White Hill, once a town of 1,200, looking west.

Maps

Township, range, and section co-ordinates are included for each map, enabling the serious ghost town explorer to locate the towns on standard base maps.

MAP 1

Legend

▬▬▬ Interstate Highway or Major Route

▬▬▬ Secondary Road: paved, fully maintained, or stone road

▪▪▪▪▪▪▪ Improved Road: gravel, stone, or soil sur-faced road

· · · · Unimproved Road

═ ═ ┊ Primitive Road

▬▬▬ State Route

▬▬▬ Interstate Route

▬▬▬ U.S. Highway

▓▓▓ Reservation or Military Restricted Area Boundary

Co-ordinates

Cerbat: SE¼, Sec. 7, T.22N., T.17W.
Frisco: Sec. 7, T.21N., R.20W.
Germa: Sec. 21, T.19N., R.20W.
Golconda: Sec. 6, T.22N., R.17W.
Gold Basin: NE¼, Sec. 13, T.28N., R.18W.
Goldflat: Approx. Sec. 18, T.20N., R.17W.
Goldroad: S½, Sec. 11, T.19N., R.20W.
Hardyville: NE¼, Sec. 16, T.20N., R.22W.
Katherine: SW¼, Sec. 5, T.21N., R.21W.
Mineral Park: N½, Sec. 24, T.23N., R.18W.
Mohave City: E½, Sec. 9, T.19N., R.22W.
Oatman: NW¼, Sec. 23, T.19N., R.20W.
Oldtrails: NE¼, Sec. 27, T.19N., R.20W.
Polhamus Landing: W½, Sec. 19, T.21N., R.21W.
Stockton: W½, Sec. 10, T.22N., R.17W.
White Hills: Sec. 14, T.27N., R.20W.

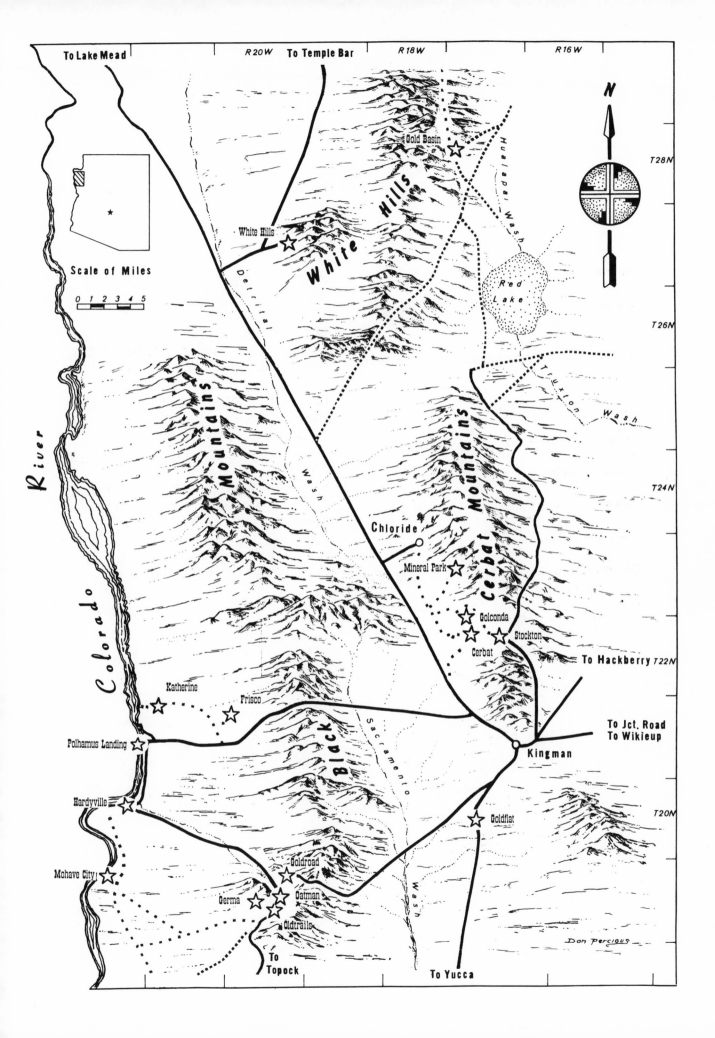

To Lake Mead

R 20 W   To Temple Bar   R 18 W   R 16 W

N

T 28 N

Scale of Miles

0 1 2 3 4 5

Gold Basin

White Hills

White Hills

Hualapai Wash

Red Lake

T 26 N

River

Detrital

Mohave Mountains

Wash

Truxton Wash

Chloride

Cerbat Mountains

T 24 N

Mineral Park

Colorado

Golconda

Stockton

Cerbat

To Hackberry T 22 N

Katherine

Frisco

Black

Sacramento

To Jct. Road
To Wikieup

Polhamus Landing

Kingman

Hardyville

Goldflat

T 20 N

Mohave City

Goldroad

Germa

Oatman

Wash

Oldtrails

Don Percious

To
Topock

To Yucca

MAP 2

Legend

▬▬▬ Interstate Highway or Major Route

▬▬ Secondary Road: paved, fully maintained, or stone road

▪▪▪▪▪▪▪ Improved Road: gravel, stone, or soil surfaced road

· · · · Unimproved Road

═ ═ ┊ Primitive Road

▬▬ State Route

▬▬▬ Interstate Route

▬▬ U.S. Highway

▓▓▓ Reservation or Military Restricted Area Boundary

Co-ordinates

Alamo Crossing: E½, Sec. 23, T.11N., R.13W.
Aubrey Landing: Approx. Sec. 9, T.11N., R.18W.
Cedar: Sec. 1, T.16N., R.15W.
Eagle Landing: Approx. Sec. 1, T.10N., R.19W.
Ehrenberg: NW¼, Sec. 15, T.3N., R.22W.
Greenwood City: Approx. Sec. 35, T.14N., R.13W.
Harqua Hala: SW¼, Sec. 21, T.4N., R.13W.
Harrisburg: NW¼, Sec. 32, T.5N., R.12W.
La Paz: Approx. Sec. 18, T.4N., R.21W.
Liverpool Landing: Approx. Sec. 16, T.13N., R.20W.
McCracken Mine: Sec. 19, T.13N., R.14W.
Owens: Approx. Sec. 12, T.15N., R.13W.
Planet: N½, Sec. 36, T.11N., R.17W.
Signal: Sec. 16, T.13N., R.13W.
Swansea: SW¼, Sec. 29, T.10N., R.15W.
Virginia City: Sec. 16, T.13N., R.13W.

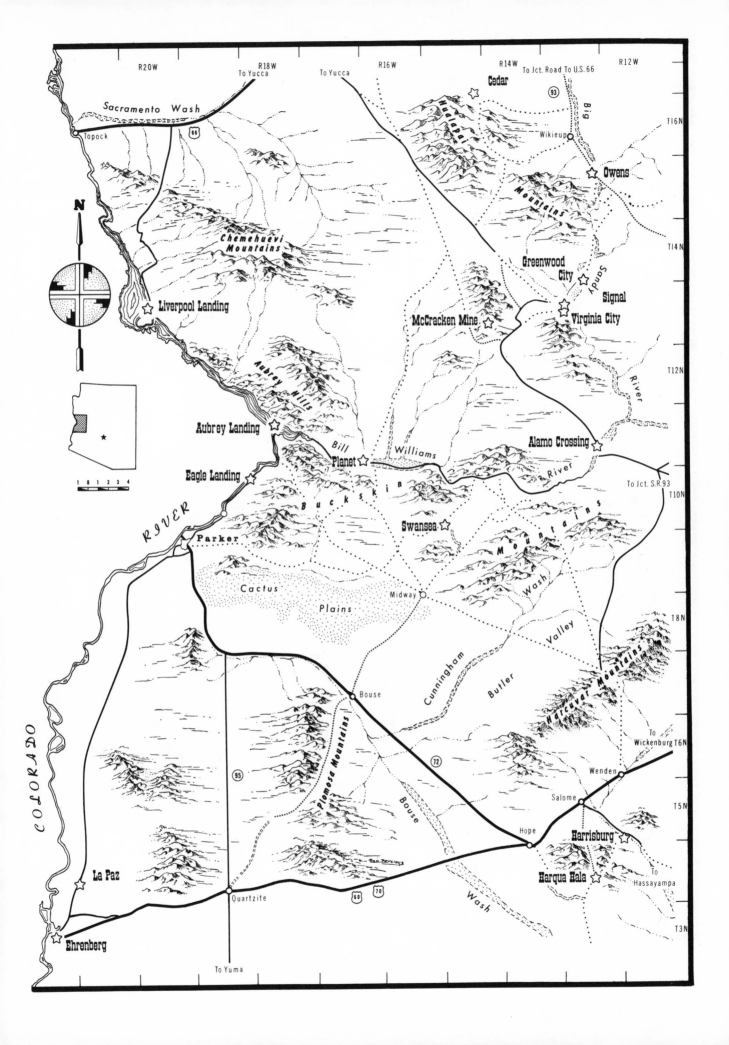

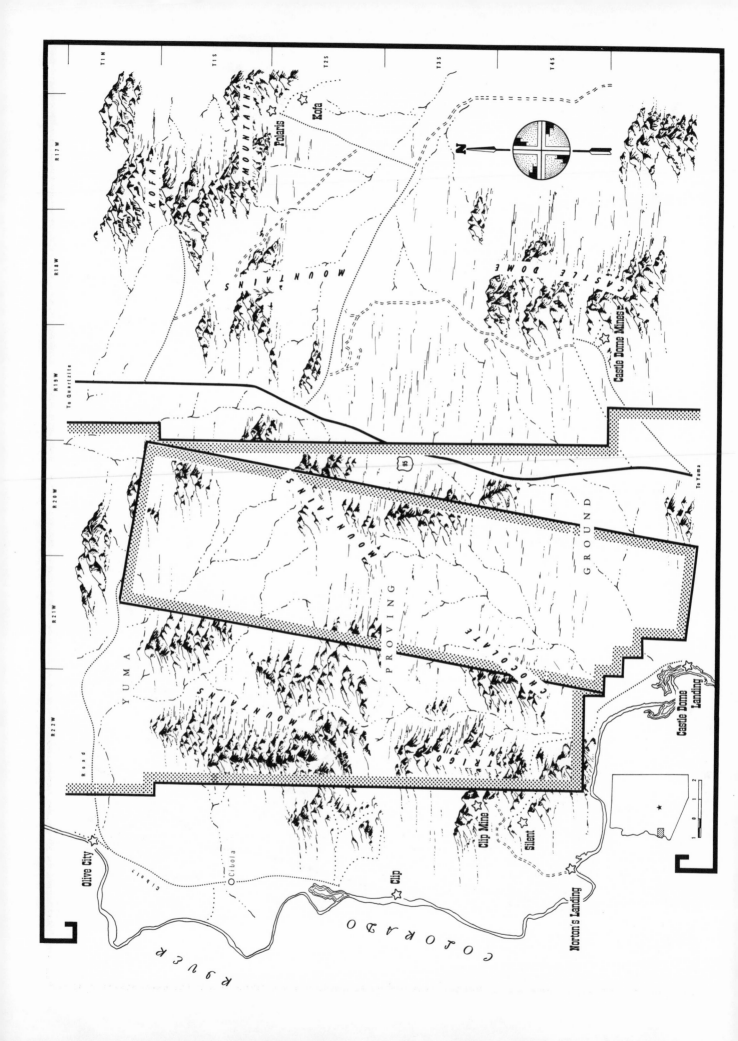

MAP 3

Co-ordinates

Castle Dome Landing: NE¼, Sec. 30, T.5S., R.21W.

Castle Dome Mines: SE¼, Sec. 35, T.4S., R.19W.

Clip: NW¼, Sec. 7, E.3S., R. 23W.

Clip Mine: NW¼, Sec. 36, T.3S., R.23W.

Kofa: E½, Sec. 12, T.2S., R.17W.

Norton's Landing: NE¼, Sec. 29, T.4S., R.23W.

Olive City: Approx. T.1N., R.23W.

Polaris: SW¼, Sec. 36, T.1S., R.17W.

Silent: Sec. 11, T.4S., R.23W.

Legend

Interstate Highway or Major Route

Secondary Road: paved, fully maintained, or stone road

Improved Road: gravel, stone, or soil sur-faced road

Unimproved Road

Primitive Road

State Route

Interstate Route

U.S. Highway

Reservation or Military Restricted Area Boundary

MAP 4

Legend

▬▬ Interstate Highway or Major Route

▬▬ Secondary Road: paved, fully maintained, or stone road

······ Improved Road: gravel, stone, or soil sur-faced road

· · · · Unimproved Road

═ ═: Primitive Road

▬▬ State Route

▬▬ Interstate Route

▬▬ U.S. Highway

▨▨ Reservation or Military Restricted Area Boundary

Co-ordinates

Fortuna: NW¼, T.10S., R.20W.
Gila City: N½, Sec. 11, T.8S., R.21W.

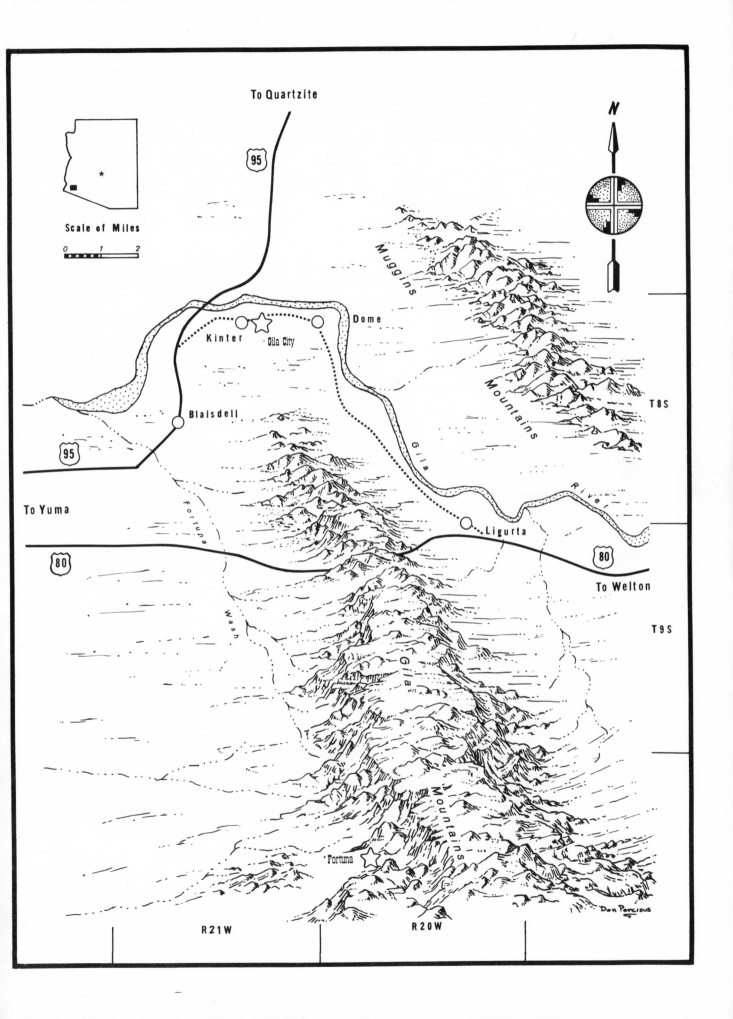

To Quartzite

95

Scale of Miles
0   1   2

Muggins

Dome

Kinter   Gila City

Blaisdell

95

To Yuma

Mountains

T 8 S

Gila

River

80

Ligurta

80

To Welton

Fortuna

Wash

T 9 S

Gila

Mountains

Fortuna

Don Percious

R 21 W   R 20 W

MAP 5

Legend

▬▬▬ Interstate Highway or Major Route

▬▬▬ Secondary Road: paved, fully maintained, or stone road

········ Improved Road: gravel, stone, or soil sur-
faced road

· · · · Unimproved Road

= = ꞉ Primitive Road

▬▬▬ State Route

▬▬▬ Interstate Route

▬▬▬ U.S. Highway

▓▓▓ Reservation or Military Restricted Area
Boundary

Co-ordinates

Congress: Sec. 22, T.10N., R.6W.
Constellation: NE¼ , Sec. 5, T.8N., R.3W.
Octave: Sec. 6, T.9N., R.4W.
Seymour: Approx. Sec. 22, or Sec. 27, T.6N.,
R.4W.
Stanton: N½ , Sec. 36, T.10N., R.5W.
Vulture City: E½ , Sec. 36, T.6N., R.6W.
Weaver: Sec. 32, T.10N., R.4W.

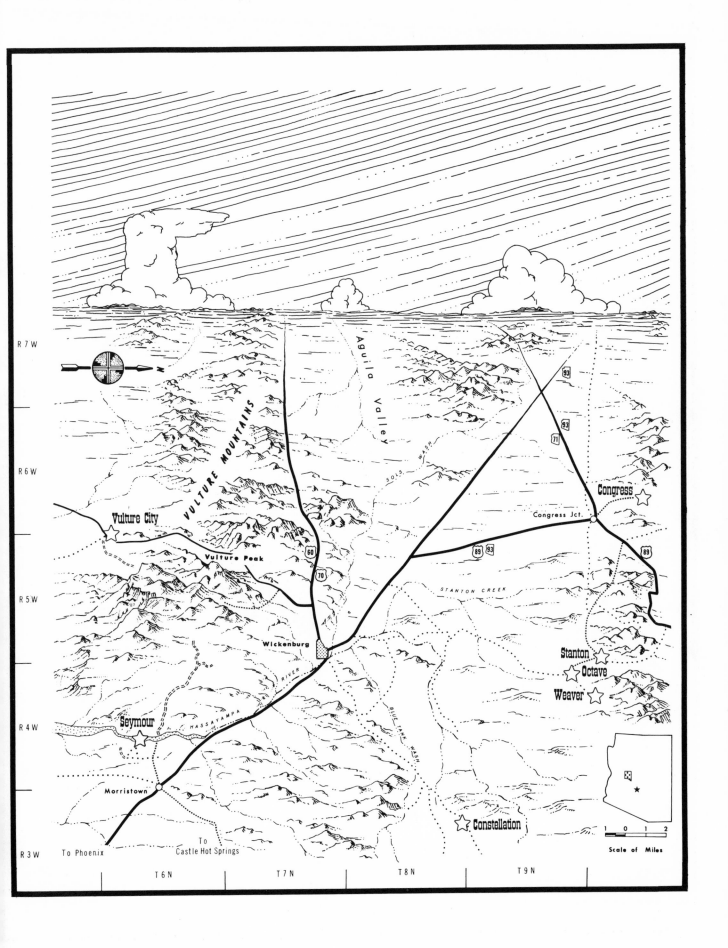

R 7 W

R 6 W

R 5 W

R 4 W

R 3 W

N

VULTURE MOUNTAINS

Aguila Valley

SOLS WASH

Vulture City

Vulture Peak

Congress

Congress Jct.

Wickenburg

STANTON CREEK

Stanton
Octave
Weaver

BLUE TANK WASH

RIVER

HASSAYAMPA

Seymour

Morristown

To Phoenix

To
Castle Hot Springs

Constellation

60

70

89   93

93

93

71

89

Scale of Miles

1   0   1   2

T 6 N

T 7 N

T 8 N

T 9 N

MAP 6

Legend

▮ Interstate Highway or Major Route

▬ Secondary Road: paved, fully maintained, or stone road

······· Improved Road: gravel, stone, or soil sur-faced road

· · · · Unimproved Road

═ ═ ═ Primitive Road

▬ State Route

▮ Interstate Route

▬ U.S. Highway

▨ Reservation or Military Restricted Area Boundary

Co-ordinates

Allen: SW¼, T.15S., R.2E.
Clarkston: NE¼, Sec. 23, T.12S., R.6W.
Gunsight: SE¼, Sec. 16, T.14S., R.4W.
Quijotoa: E½, Sec. 12, T.15S., R.2E.
Sasco: W½, Sec. 21, T.10S., R.9E.
Silverbell: SE¼, Sec. 33, T.11S., R.8E.
Vekol: N½, Sec. 34, T.9S., R.2E.

MAP 7

Legend

▬▬▬ Interstate Highway or Major Route

▬▬▬ Secondary Road: paved, fully maintained, or stone road

▪▪▪▪▪▪ Improved Road: gravel, stone, or soil surfaced road

▪ ▪ ▪ ▪ Unimproved Road

= =: Primitive Road

▬▬▬ State Route

▬▬▬ Interstate Route

▬▬▬ U.S. Highway

▓▓▓ Reservation or Military Restricted Area Boundary

Co-ordinates

Cherry: SE¼, Sec. 17, T.14N., R.3E.
Jerome: T.16N., R.2E.

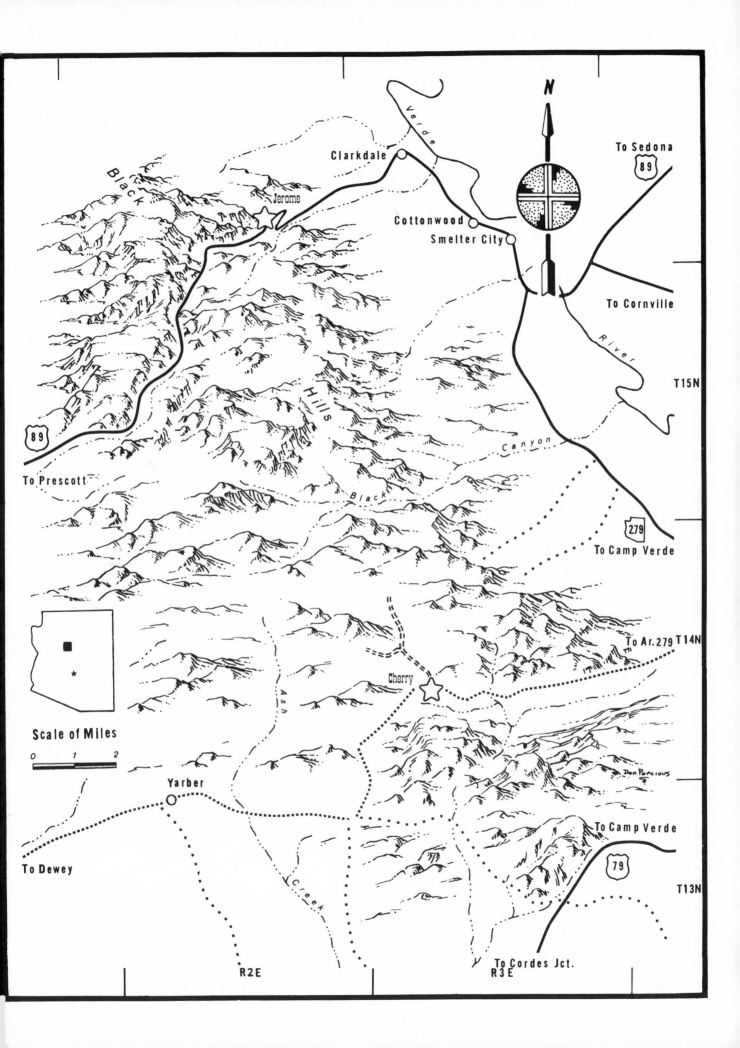

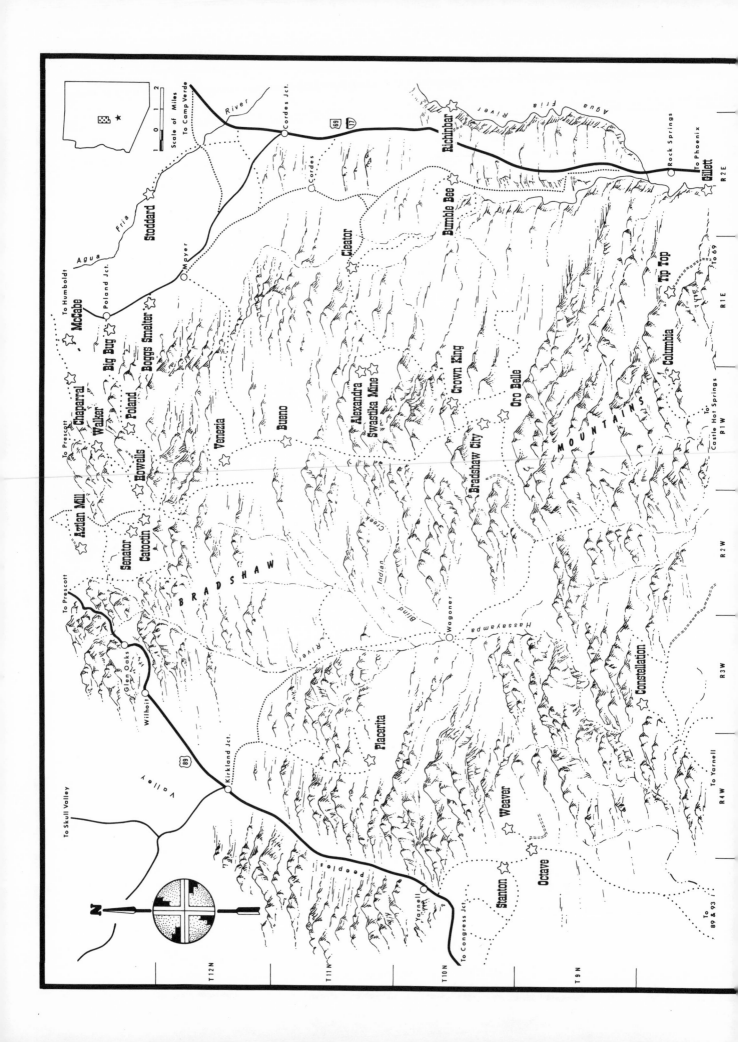

MAP 8

Legend

▬ Interstate Highway or Major Route

▬ Secondary Road: paved, fully maintained, or stone road

⋯⋯ Improved Road: gravel, stone, or soil sur-faced road

· · · · Unimproved Road

= = : Primitive Road

▬ State Route

▬ Interstate Route

▬ U.S. Highway

▓▒ Reservation or Military Restricted Area Boundary

Co-ordinates

Alexandra: T.11N., R.1W.
Aztlan Mill: Approx. Sec. 28, T.13N., R.2W.
Big Bug: N½, Sec. 5, T.12N., R.1E.
Boggs Smelter: Sec. 16, T.12N., R.1E.
Bradshaw City: Sec. 27, T.10N., R.1W.
Bueno: T.11N., R.1W.
Bumble Bee: Sec. 33, T.10N., R.2E.
Catoctin: T.12½N., R.2W.
Chaparral: S½, Sec. 25, T.13N., R.1W.
Cleator: T.10N., R.1E.
Columbia: Sec. 12, T.8N., R.1W.
Constellation: NE¼, Sec. 5, T.8N., R.3W.
Crown King: T.10N., R.1W.
Gillett: Sec. 21, T.8N., R.2E.
Howells: T.12½N., R.2W.
McCabe: NW¼, Sec. 29, T.13N., R.1E.
Octave: Sec. 6, T.9N., R.4W.
Oro Belle: T.10N., R.1W.
Placerita: SE¼, Sec. 26, T.11N., R.4W.
Poland: T.12N., R.1W.
Richinbar: E½, Sec. 36, T.10N., R.2E.
Senator: T.12N., R.2W.
Stanton: N½, Sec. 36, T.10N., R.5W.
Stoddard: NE¼, Sec. 17, T.12N., R2E.
Swastika Mine: T.11N., R.1W.
Tip Top: Sec. 10, T.8N., R.1E.
Venezia: T.12N., R.2E.
Walker: SW¼, Sec. 33, T.13N., R.1W.
Weaver: Sec. 32, T.10N., R.4W.

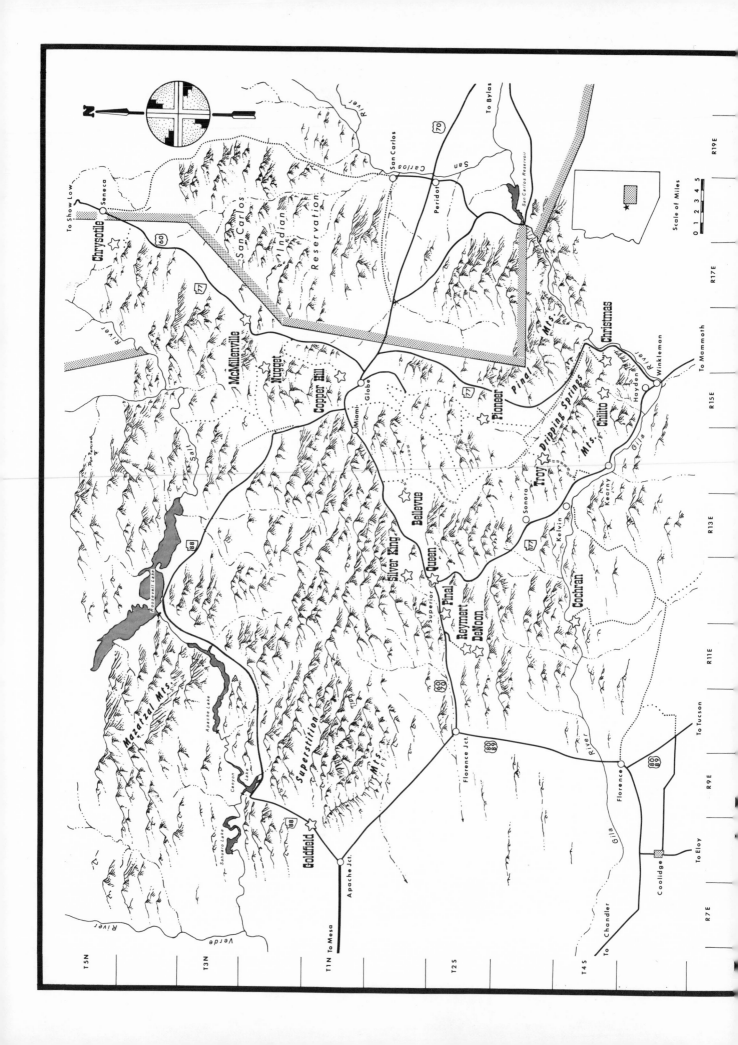

MAP 9

Legend

▮ Interstate Highway or Major Route

— Secondary Road: paved, fully maintained, or stone road

•••••• Improved Road: gravel, stone, or soil surfaced road

· · · · Unimproved Road

═ ═ ═ Primitive Road

— State Route

▮ Interstate Route

— U.S. Highway

▦ Reservation or Military Restricted Area Boundary

Co-ordinates

Bellevue: SW¼, Sec. 17, T.1S., R.14E.
Chilito: NE¼, Sec. 27, T.4S., R.15E.
Christmas: NE¼, Sec. 30, T.4S., R.16E.
Chrysotile: T.4N., R.17E.
Cochran: N½, Sec. 7, T.4S., R.12E.
Copper Hill: SW¼, Sec. 15, T.1N., R.15½ E.
DeNoon: N½, Sec. 27, T.2S., R.11E.
Goldfield: W½, Sec. 1, T.1N., R.8E.
McMillenville: T.3N., R.16E.
Nugget: T.2N., R.15½E.
Pinal: NW¼, Sec. 8, T.2S., R.12E.
Pioneer: NW¼, Sec. 29, T.2S., R.15E.
Queen: SW¼, Sec. 36, T.1S., R.12E.
Reymert: NE¼, Sec. 22, T.2S., R.11E.
Silver King: W½, Sec. 24, T.1S., R.12E.
Troy: SE¼, Sec. 22, T.3S., R.14E.

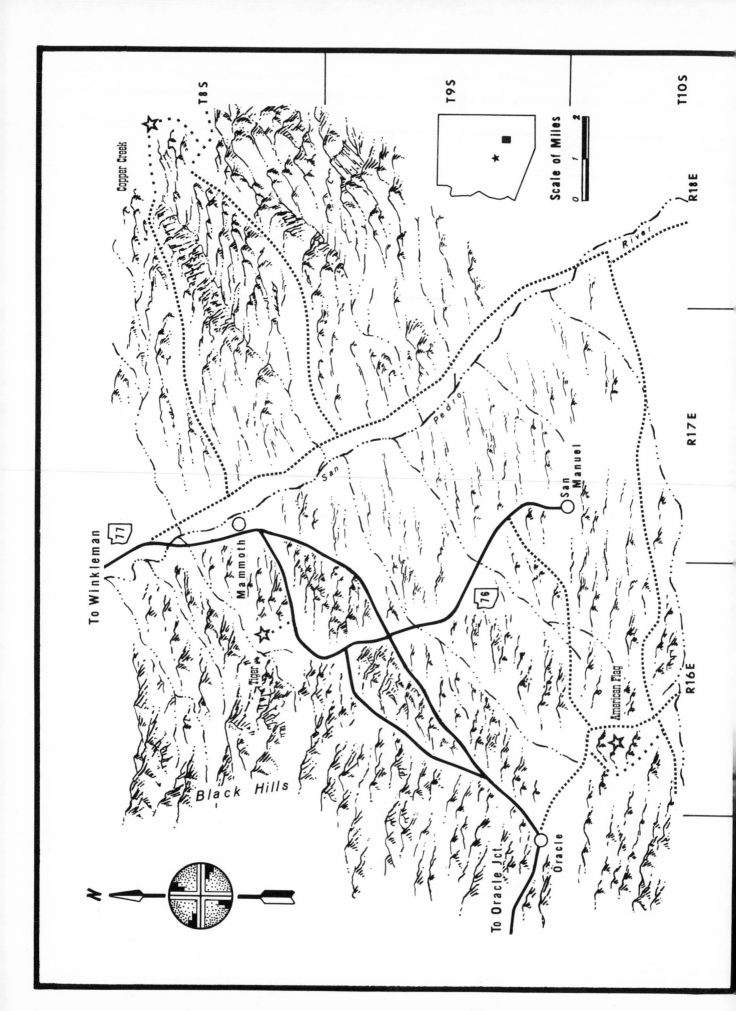

MAP 10

Legend

▬ Interstate Highway or Major Route

▬ Secondary Road: paved, fully maintained, or stone road

⋯ Improved Road: gravel, stone, or soil surfaced road

⋅ ⋅ ⋅ ⋅ Unimproved Road

=ᴉ= Primitive Road

▬ State Route

▬ Interstate Route

▬ U.S. Highway

▓ Reservation or Military Restricted Area Boundary

Co-ordinates

American Flag: Approx. NE¼, Sec. 8, T.10S., R.16E.

Copper Creek: W½, Sec. 11, T.8S., R.18E.

Tiger: W½, Sec. 26, T.8S., R.16E.

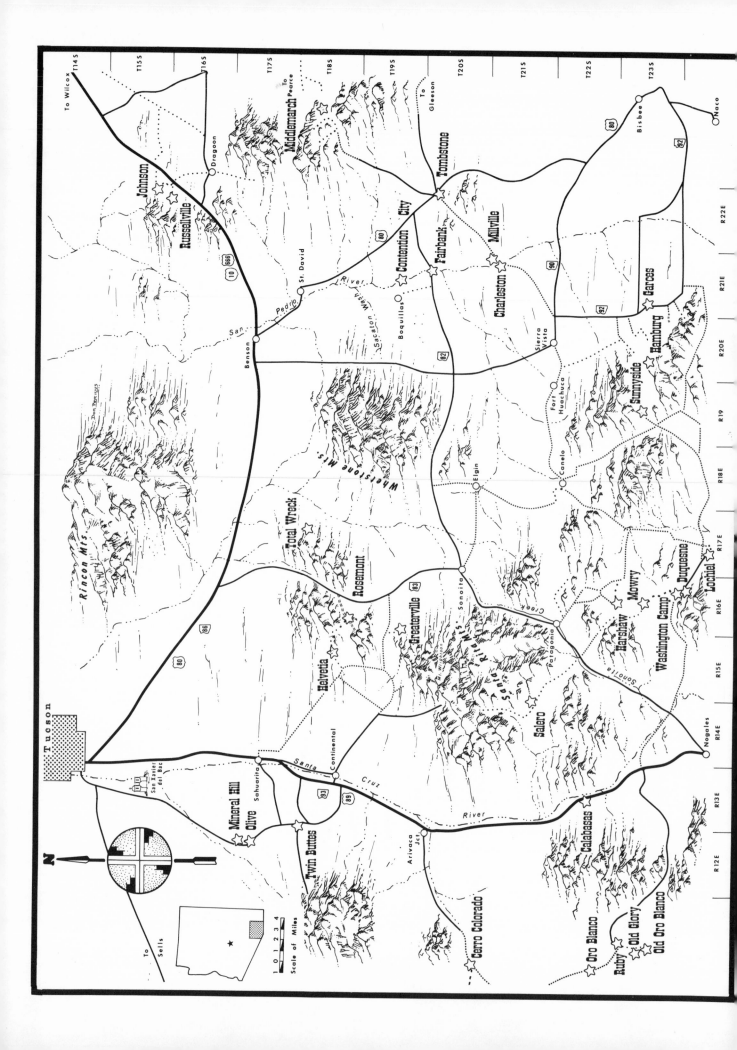

MAP 11

Legend

▬ Interstate Highway or Major Route

— Secondary Road: paved, fully maintained, or stone road

···· Improved Road: gravel, stone, or soil sur-faced road

· · · · Unimproved Road

= = = Primitive Road

— State Route

▬ Interstate Route

▬ U.S. Highway

▓▒ Reservation or Military Restricted Area Boundary

Co-ordinates

Calabasas: T.22S., R.13E.
Cerro Colorado: E½, Sec. 25, T.20S., R.10E.
Charleston: SE¼, Sec. 2, T.21S., R.21E.
Contention City: Sec. 21, T.19S., R.21E.
Duquesne: T.24S., R.16E.
Fairbank: Sec. 3, T.20S., R.21E.
Garces: SW¼, Sec. 17, T.23S., R.21E.
Gleeson: SE¼, Sec. 31, T.19S., R.25E.
Greaterville: SW¼, Sec. 19, T.19S., R.16E.
Hamburg: SE¼, Sec. 17, T.23S., R.20E.
Harshaw: T.23S., R.16E.
Helvetia: NW¼, Sec. 23, T.18S., R.15E.
Johnson: E½, Sec. 26, and W½, Sec. 25, T.15N., R.22E.
Lochiel: NW¼, Sec. 21, T.24S., R.17E.
Middlemarch: SE¼, Sec. 12, T.18S., R.23E.
Millville: E½, Sec. 2, T.21S., R.21E.
Mineral Hill: N½, Sec. 2, T.17S., R.12E.
Mowry: T.23S., R.16E.
Old Glory: SE¼, Sec. 7, T.23S., R.11E.
Old Oro Blanco: SW¼, Sec. 17, T.23S., R.11E.
Olive: N½, Sec. 11, T.17S., R.12E.
Oro Blanco: SW¼, Sec. 24, T.22S., R.10E.
Rosemont: SW¼, Sec. 29, T.18S., R.16E.
Ruby: NE¼, Sec. 5, T.23N., R.11E.
Russellville: SW¼, Sec. 35, T.15S., R.22E.
Salero: NE¼, Sec. 25, T.21S., R.14E.
Sunnyside: NW¼, Sec. 15, T.23S., R.19E.
Tombstone: NE¼, Sec. 11, T.20S., R.22E.
Total Wreck: SE¼, Sec. 3, T.18S., R.17E.
Twin Buttes: Sec. 31, T.17S., R.13E.
Washington Camp: T.24S., R.16E.

MAP 12

Legend

▬▬▬ Interstate Highway or Major Route

▬▬▬ Secondary Road: paved, fully maintained, or stone road

▪▪▪▪▪▪▪ Improved Road: gravel, stone, or soil sur-faced road

· · · · Unimproved Road

＝＝: Primitive Road

▬▬▬ State Route

▬▬▬ Interstate Route

▬▬▬ U.S. Highway

▓▓▓ Reservation or Military Restricted Area Boundary

Co-ordinates

Metcalf: S½ , Sec. 4, T.4S., R.29E.

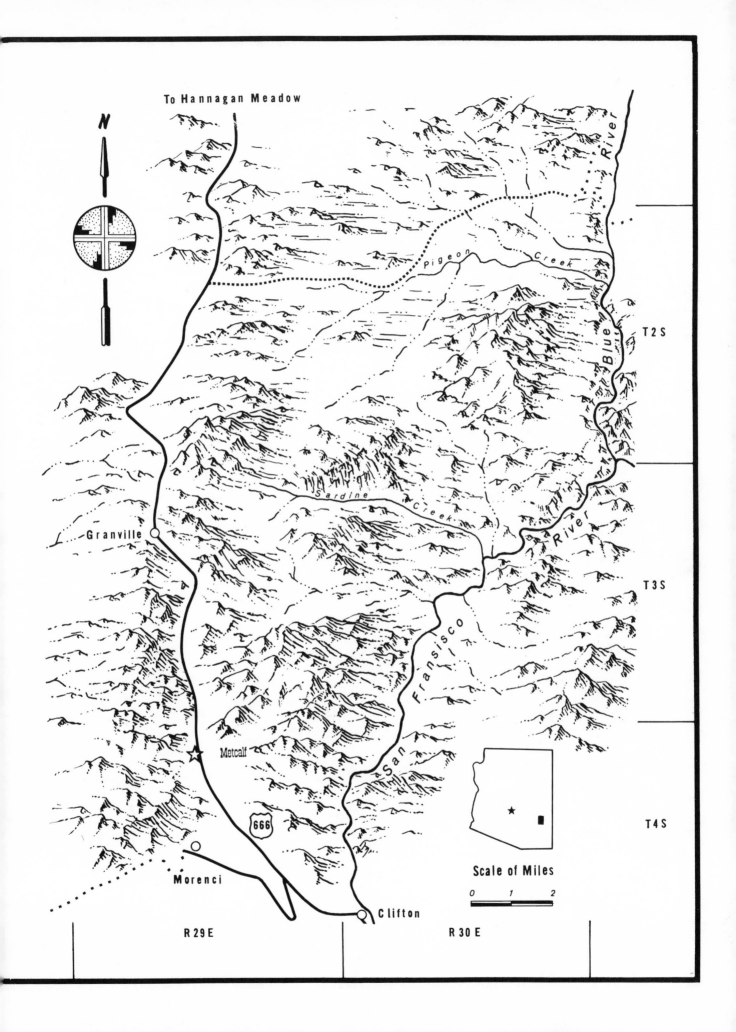

To Hannagan Meadow

N

Blue River

Pigeon Creek

T 2 S

Sardine Creek

Granville

San Fransisco River

T 3 S

Metcalf

666

T 4 S

Morenci

Clifton

Scale of Miles

0   1   2

R 29 E

R 30 E

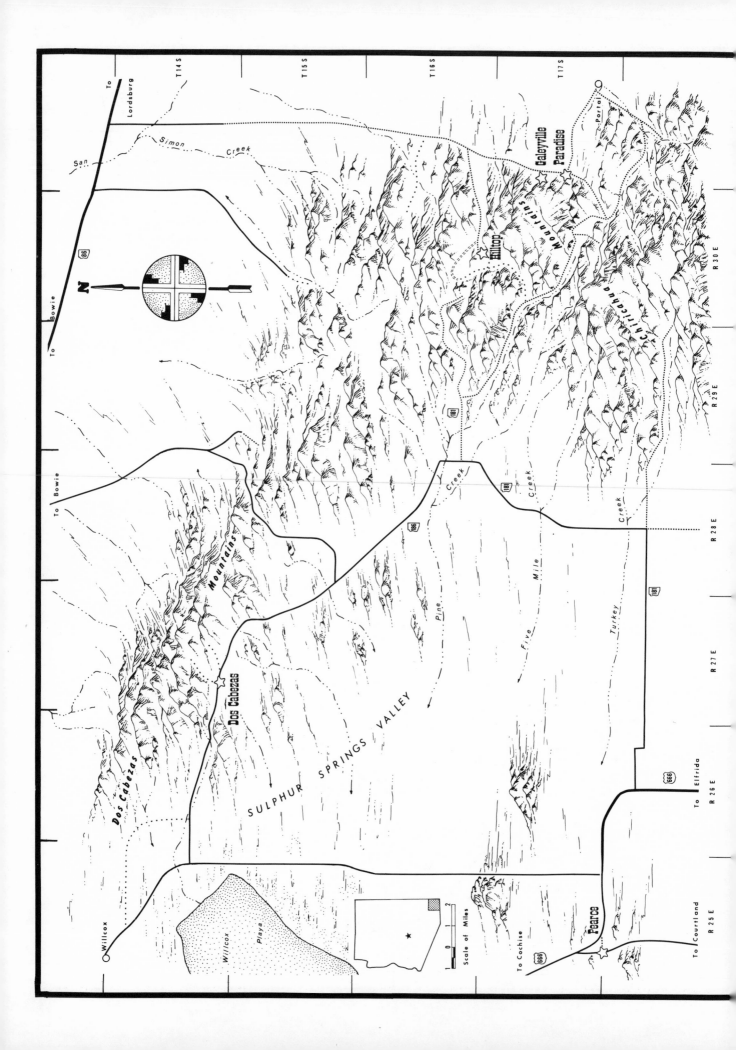

MAP 13

Legend

▮ Interstate Highway or Major Route

▬ Secondary Road: paved, fully maintained, or stone road

⋯ Improved Road: gravel, stone, or soil sur-faced road

⋅⋅⋅⋅ Unimproved Road

= = : Primitive Road

▬ State Route

▮ Interstate Route

▬ U.S. Highway

▓ Reservation or Military Restricted Area Boundary

Co-ordinates

Courtland: NW¼, Sec. 21, T.19S., R. 25E.
Dos Cabezas: N½, Sec. 32, T.14S., R.27E.
Galeyville: NW¼, Sec. 19, T.17N., R.31E.
Hilltop: E½, Sec. 33, T.16S., R.30E.
Paradise: W½, Sec. 19, T.17S., R.31E.
Pearce: N½, Sec. 5, T.18S., R.25E.

Selected Bibliography

Adams, Ward R. and Richard E. Sloan. *History of Arizona*. Vols. I–IV, Phoenix, Record Publishing Co., 1930.

Arizona: A State Guide ("American Guide Series") New York, Hastings House, 1940.

Arizona Business Directory 1905–1906. Vol. I. Denver, The Gazetteer Publishing Co., 1907.

Arizona Business Directory 1909–1910. Vol. III. Denver, The Gazeteer Publishing Co., 1909.

Arizona State Business Directory 1911–1912. Vol. IV. Denver, The Gazetteer Publishing Co., 1911.

Arizona State Business Directory 1914–1915. Vol. IV. Denver, The Gazetteer Publishing Co., 1914.

Arizona State Business Directory 1925. Vol. XVI. Denver, The Gazeteer Publishing and Printing Co.

Arizona State Business Directory 1930. Vol. XXI. Denver, The Gazetteer Publishing and Printing Co.

Barnes, Will C. *Arizona Place Names*. University of Arizona *General Bulletin* No. 2, Tucson, University of Arizona, 1935.

————. *Arizona Place Names*. Revised and enlarged by Byrd H. Granger. Tucson, University of Arizona Press, 1960.

Breckenridge, William M. *Helldorado*. Boston and New York, Houghton Mifflin Company, 1928.

Brown, J. Cabel. *Calabazas or Amusing Recollections of An Arizona "City."* San Francisco, Valleau & Peterson, 1892.

Browne, J. Ross. *A Tour Through Arizona, 1864*. New York, Harper Brothers, 1869.

Bryan, Kirk. *Papago Country, Arizona*. Water Supply Paper No. 499. Washington, Government Printing Office, 1925.

Cleland, Robert Glass. *A History of Phelps Dodge 1834–1950*. New York, Alfred A. Knopf, 1952.

Colorado, New Mexico, Utah, Nevada, Wyoming and Arizona Gazetteer and Business Directory 1884–5. Chicago and Detroit, R. L. Polk & Co. and A. C. Danser.

Dunbar, Alexander R. (ed.). *International Mining Manual 1907*. Denver, Western Mining Directory Co.

Dunning, Charles H. and Edward H. Peplow, Jr. *Rock to Riches*. Phoenix, Southwest Publishing Company, Inc., c. 1959.

Elliot, Wallace W. *History of Arizona Territory*, San Francisco, Wallace W. Elliot and Co., 1884.

Elsing, Morris J. and Robert E. S. Heneman. *Arizona Metal Production*. Arizona Bureau of Mines, *Bulletin 140*. Tucson, University of Arizona, 1936.

Farish, Thomas Edwin. *History of Arizona*. Vols. I–VIII. Phoenix [n.p.], 1915.

Hamilton, Patrick. *The Resources of Arizona*. Second edition. San Francisco, A. L. Bancroft & Co., 1883.

Hand-Book of Tucson and Surroundings 1880. Tucson, A.T., T. R. Serin, Publisher.

Hill, James M. *Mining Districts of Western States*. U.S. Geological Survey *Bulletin 507*. Washington, Government Printing Office, 1912.

Hinton, Richard J. *The Handbook to Arizona*. San Francisco, Payot, Upham & Company, 1878. Republished by Arizona Silhouettes, Tucson, 1954.

Hodge, Hiram C. *Arizona as It Is, or The Coming Country*. New York, Hurd and Houghton, 1877.

International Mining Manual 1915. Denver, The Western Mining Directory Co.

Lindgren, Waldemar. *Ore Deposits of the Jerome and Bradshaw Mountains Quadrangles, Ariz*. U.S. Geological Survey *Bulletin 782*. Washington, Government Printing Office, 1926.

Lockwood, Frank C. *Pioneer Days In Arizona*. New York, The Macmillan Company, 1932.

McClintock, James H. *Arizona: Prehistoric: Aboriginal: Pioneer: Modern*. Vol. I–III. Chicago, S. J. Clarke Publishing Company, 1916.

McKenney's Business Directory of the Principal Towns of Central and Southern California, Arizona, New Mexico, Southern Colorado and Kansas 1882–3. Oakland and San Francisco, Pacific Press.

McKenney's Pacific Coast Directory for 1880–1. San Francisco, L. M. McKenney & Co.

Miller, Joseph. *Arizona: The Last Frontier*. New York, Hastings House, 1956.

Murbarger, Nell. *Ghosts of the Adobe Walls*. Los Angeles 41, Westernlore Press, 1964.

Myers, John. *The Last Chance: Tombstone's Early Years*. New York, E. P. Dutton & Company, Inc., 1950.

Peck, Anne Merriman. *The March of Arizona*

History. Tucson, Arizona Silhouettes, 1962.

Pumpelly, Raphael. *My Reminiscences.* Vol. I. New York, Henry Holt and Company, 1918.

Rockfellow, John A. *The Log of an Arizona Trail Blazer.* Tucson, Acme Printing Co., 1933.

Schrader, F. C. *Mineral Deposits of the Cerbat Range, Black Mountains, and Grand Wash Cliffs, Mohave County, Arizona.* U.S. Geological Survey *Bulletin 397.* Washington, Government Printing Office, 1909.

————. *Mineral Deposits of the Santa Rita and Patagonia Mountains, Arizona.* U.S. Geological Survey *Bulletin 582.* Washington, Government Printing Office, 1915.

Southern Pacific Coast Directory For 1888–9. San Francisco, McKenney Directory Company, 1888.

Stephens, Bascom A. *Quijotoa Mining District Guide Book.* Tucson, Citizen Printing and Publishing Company, 1884.

Theobald, John and Lillian. *Arizona Territory Post Offices & Postmasters.* Phoenix, The Arizona Historical Foundation, 1961.

United States Annual Mining Review and Stock Ledger for 1879. New York, 1879.

Walters, Lorenzo D. *Tombstone's Yesterday.* Tucson, Acme Printing Co., 1928.

Wilson, Eldred D. *Geology and Ore Deposits of the Courtland Gleeson Region.* Arizona Bureau of Mines *Bulletin 123.* Tucson, University of Arizona, 1927.

————. *Asbestos Deposits of Arizona.* Arizona Bureau of Mines *Bulletin 126.* Tucson, University of Arizona, 1928.

————. *Geology and Mineral Deposits of Southern Yuma County, Arizona.* Arizona Bureau of Mines *Bulletin 135.* Tucson, University of Arizona, 1933.

————. *Arizona Gold Placers.* Arizona Bureau of Mines *Bulletin 135.* Tucson, University of Arizona, 1933.

————. *Arizona Zinc and Lead Deposits Part I.* Arizona Bureau of Mines *Bulletin 156.* Tucson, University of Arizona, 1950.

————. *Arizona Zinc and Lead Deposits Part II.* Arizona Bureau of Mines *Bulletin 158.* Tucson, University of Arizona, 1951.

————. *Gold Placers and Placering in Arizona.* Arizona Bureau of Mines *Bulletin 168.* Tucson, University of Arizona, 1961.

————, J. B. Cunningham and G. M. Butler. *Arizona Lode Gold Mines and Gold Mining.* Arizona Bureau of Mines *Bulletin 137.* Tucson, University of Arizona, 1934.

Wolle, Muriel Sibell. *The Bonanza Trail.* Bloomington, Indiana University Press, 1953.

Index

GHOST TOWNS OF ARIZONA was set on the Linotype in eleven-point Times Roman, the distinctive typeface designed by Stanley Morison for use in *The Times* of London.

The page-by-page layout for *Ghost Towns of Arizona* was made by the authors themselves, and the book was printed by offset lithography from negatives prepared at the University of Oklahoma Press.

UNIVERSITY OF OKLAHOMA PRESS

NORMAN